60¢

DEN LEADERSHIP

This book is designed to help you, the leader of a den, do the job you've agreed to do — run a Cub Scout den. It will help you learn your job quickly and how to do it as efficiently as possible.

Parts I and II will give you the information on what Cub Scouting is about and how a den works.

The rest of the book is full of resources on pack meetings, planning, advancement, uniforms, working with other leaders, and the philosophy of Cub Scouting.

Since Cub Scouting has emphasized for years the use of women as Den Mothers of 8- and 9-year-olds, most of the references in this book are to them. We recognize that there are situations where men may serve as Den Leaders. Therefore, this book may be used by both men and women.

The latest information on Den Leader uniforms and training is included. Den Mothers wear the Den Mother uniform and its insignia. Male Den Leaders wear the Cub Scout leader's uniform and Den Leader insignia.

When speaking of den leadership in this book, we will use the "Den Mother" title. It should be remembered that the den leadership responsibilities are the same for Den Mothers and Den Leaders.

1971 PRINTING
Copyright 1967
BOY SCOUTS OF AMERICA
North Brunswick, New Jersey
No. 3212   Printed in U.S.A.   110M871
Library of Congress Catalog Card Number: 38-16321

DEN LEADER'S BOOK

A Manual for Adult Leaders of Cub Scout Dens

BOY SCOUTS OF AMERICA

CONTENTS

Scout advancement—use of Cub Scout Advancement Chart and den doodles to spur advancement.

YOUR OPPORTUNITY

Even though your home is one of your most treasured possessions, Cub Scouting asks you to take into it each week a lively group of boys. This adds to the confusion and noise in your home. But it adds something else, too—something which some mothers and fathers overlook as they consider the possibility of serving as Den Leaders.

There are two very different types of homes. In one type everything will always be just so. The furniture is not likely to be marred. There will be no scratches on the floors. There will be little shouting or noise except from the boy who lives in that home, and even his shouting will be subdued and experimental. His mother will seldom be troubled by the shouts and laughter of other boys, because it is not likely that they will come there.

Unless something unusual happens, that is the type of home it will always be. As the children who live in it become young men and women, the rugs will never be rolled up for social occasions. They will take their noise and laughter where it is better understood and more welcome.

THE OTHER TYPE

But there's that other type, too; the kind you probably have.

This type attracts the friends of the children who live in it. They would rather bring their friends there than join them elsewhere. It is a home where children are welcome—where they learn to take care of the furniture rather than preserve it through lack of use. It's a home which later will attract young people.

It's true, the first type of home will be peaceful—because it will be empty. Too quiet—too peaceful—too empty.

But there are other more wonderful things to be sought after in life than peace and quiet—and besides, if you live in the second type of home, it does not mean that all of your own personal comforts and pleasures must be sacrificed. Lasting satisfaction can come from the knowledge that, as each day goes by, you are guaranteeing that your children's future memories of their parents and their home will be happy ones.

Since you want the second type of home, you must start to build now. In just a year or two it will be too late. That's why Cub Scouting is not all "give" on your part. You'll "take" a finer home life for you and your children.

You are making one of the finest possible contributions to your community by serving as a Den Mother in Cub Scouting. You are not only dealing with boys, but with parents, too. You are strengthening the life of your community by enriching the lives of the families who live in it. You are teaching boys to respect their homes and their parents. You are helping parents to understand their boys better by doing things with them. Few community services are more important than this.

THE CATCHING QUALITIES

You will find serving as a Den Mother to be one of the most pleasant contributions you can make. You will be working with boys. You will find them full of anticipation and enthusiasm. Their viewpoint is fresh and sparkling. The mother who works with such raw material cannot help but catch some of these qualities herself.

It's this sparkle which must always be evident in your leadership. Do not wear your feelings too close to the surface. Keep your sense of humor. Many things that at first glance seem very serious are actually funny. If you can keep your leadership on a light-and-free level, it is likely that your boys will respond in the same way. Then everybody will get more fun out of Cub Scouting —and more serious benefits, too.

Of course, there will be some problems along the way. But you will find more than enough satisfaction to balance them. You'll get to know your own boys better. You'll be making the sort of home you would like to have. You'll be building the life of your community. As you do these things your faith in other folks will increase as you see them working together on behalf of your boys.

Welcome to leadership in Cub Scouting—your opportunity.

PART I
YOU AND YOUR DEN

1. WHAT CUB SCOUTING IS ALL ABOUT

What is Cub Scouting, anyway?

I s it a baby-sitting service? Is it some sort of organized play group for boys? Is it just a program in which boys learn a few games and crafts to occupy their idle hours?

No, no, and no! Cub Scouting is much, much more. At the outset of your service as a Den Mother, you would do well to get clear in your mind just what Cub Scouting is.

Simply put, Cub Scouting is a home- and neighborhood-centered program which parents, leaders, and institutions use to help in the growth and development of boys from 8 to 11 years old. The program was developed by the Boy Scouts of America to support its broad objectives of character development, citizenship training, and mental and physical fitness. These have been restated and expanded to help everyone understand how Cub Scouting's methods (program and procedure) seek to effect these objectives for Cub Scout-age boys. You must understand them and bear in mind these real aims of Cub Scouting as you work with your boys if you are to be effective.

THE PURPOSE OF CUB SCOUTING

Cub Scouting is a program of the Boy Scouts of America for parents, leaders, and institutions to use with boys 8, 9, and 10 years of age for the purpose of:

- ♦ Influencing the development of the boys' character and spiritual growth.
- ♦ Developing habits and attitudes of good citizenship.
- ♦ Encouraging good sportsmanship and pride in growing strong in mind and body.
- ♦ Improving understanding within the family.
- ♦ Strengthening the ability to get along with other boys and to respect other people.

- Fostering a sense of personal achievement by developing new interests and skills.
- Showing how to be helpful and do one's best.
- Providing fun and exciting new things to do.
- Preparing boys to become Boy Scouts.

These are the goals toward which you will strive as a Den Mother. It goes without saying that all of this is in the background as you work with your Cub Scouts. You can't be solemn and serious in working with boys, but as long as you are aware of the goals of Cub Scouting, they will affect everything you do with your Cub Scouts.

So far as the boys are concerned, Cub Scouting is fun and high adventure. If it isn't that, they quickly lose interest. But as you provide the fun and adventure, keep in the back of your mind the thought that behind the fun there is a serious purpose.

CUB SCOUTING'S METHODS

If you are new to Cub Scouting, it may be helpful first to take a quick view of the whole picture. How does Cub Scouting work and how does the Den Mother fit in?

Let's start with the boy. He may join Cub Scouting when he is 8 years old or in the third grade. He joins the pack because he wants to share in the fun.

He is assigned to a den, probably one comprised of boys from his own neighborhood. If he is 10, he joins a Webelos den, which is for 10-year-olds only and under the leadership of a man.

In your den, therefore, you will be working with boys under 10 years old. Chances are you will have five to eight of these 8- and 9-year-old boys under your wing. Another mother is recruited to help as your assistant.

Working with you as your activity assistant will be a den chief, who is a Boy Scout. One of your Cub Scouts will be elected as the boy leader of the den. He will be known as the denner, and he will help you and the den chief.

Your den will also have a den dad, the father of one of your Cub Scouts, who will cooperate with you in such ways as taking boys on special outings, building items you may need, and obtain-

```
                    INSTITUTION
             INSTITUTIONAL REPRESENTATIVE
                  PACK COMMITTEE
    ────────────────────────────────────────
               Members of Institution
    Den Dads — Webelos Den Dads — Members at Large
    ────────────────────────────────────────
                    Chairman
```

CUBMASTER

```
ASST. CUBMASTER          WEBELOS DEN LEADER        WEBELOS DEN LEADER
 (One or More)                WEBELOS                  WEBELOS
                               Den 1                    DEN 2
                         ─────────────────        ─────────────────
                         Assistant Webelos        Assistant Webelos
                            Den Leader               Den Leader
                               Dads                     Dads
                             Den Chief                Den Chief
                          Webelos Denner           Webelos Denner
                          Webelos Scouts           Webelos Scouts
```

DEN LEADER COACH

*DEN MOTHER	DEN MOTHER	DEN MOTHER	DEN MOTHER
Den 1	Den 2	Den 3	Den 4
Asst. Den Mother	Asst. Den Mother	Asst. Den Mother	Asst. Den Mother
Den Dad	Den Dad	Den Dad	Den Dad
Den Chief	Den Chief	Den Chief	Den Chief
Denner	Denner	Denner	Denner
Cub Scouts	Cub Scouts	Cub Scouts	Cub Scouts

*Cub Scouting emphasizes the use of women as Den Mothers for the leadership of Cub Scout dens for 8- and 9-year-olds. However, we recognize that there are situations where, for various reasons, men may properly serve as Cub Scout Den Leaders.

ing help and support from other fathers. He does not normally attend the den meetings, which are held once a week after school during the school year. In the summer, meetings are more informal and at different hours.

Women usually lead dens as Den Mothers. Women are usually readily available when boys come home from school. There are situations where for various reasons men serve in this capacity under the title of Den Leader.

Your den is part of a larger group called the pack. It is made up of several dens and meets once a month in the early evening under the leadership of the pack leader, called a Cubmaster. At the pack meeting, each den shows the things it has made during the month and may also present a skit or stunt.

The pack may be sponsored by a church or synagogue, PTA, service club, or some other civic group that believes in the value of Cub Scouting. The sponsor (called a chartered institution) appoints a pack committee that sets policy, names the top leaders of the pack, handles finances, and serves generally as a board of directors. Probably the den dad of your den will be a member of the pack committee.

The chartered institution is linked with the national Boy Scout organization through a man called the institutional representative. He represents your pack and institution on the district committee and serves as a member of your local council.

One of the members of your pack staff is the Den Leader coach, who will help you get started on Cub Scouting and continue to help you as long as you are a Den Mother.

The responsibilities of each of these leaders will be discussed in detail in later chapters.

FUN AND LEARNING

In briefest outline, that is the organizational picture. But there is more to Cub Scouting than merely periodic meetings of the den and pack. The program provides a continual stimulus for fun and learning for each Cub Scout. The key to this is the advancement plan. The Cub Scouts are constantly challenged to do new things, learn new skills, and play new games. This challenge comes in meeting certain requirements, called achievements and electives, in order to advance in rank. These achievements and electives, which compose the advancement plan for 8- and 9-year-old boys, include activities, skills, and projects that will help boys develop

8

physically and mentally, build self-reliance, encourage spiritual growth, grow in pride as their skill and knowledge increases, and teach them to assume responsibility, good personal habits, new hobby interests, and pride in their American heritage.

Most of your boys will enjoy tackling these requirements, because they are geared to boys' interests.

The boys' own parents approve their work on the achievements and electives, and most of this work will be done in their homes. Your job will be to spur their interest in advancing, to keep a record of their progress, and perhaps occasionally to work with them on an achievement and elective during a den meeting.

In summary, that's the Cub Scouting picture. In the next chapter, we'll get down to details.

2. HOW THE DEN WORKS

H ere's the story of Hickory Street before Cub Scouting came to it. It will help you to see more clearly the naturalness of Cub Scouting.

Hickory Street is a typical American street. Like most American streets it is filled with boys. Bob and Timmy, ages 9 and 8, live in the first house; down a few houses live 8-year-old twins, Andy and Bruce; just around the bend in the street are Eric, 8, Robby, 9, and Mike, nearly 10—seven typical American boys with the usual potential for mischief and noise.

Since these boys live near each other, it is only natural that they spend most of their time together. You'd probably call them a natural neighborhood play group. Across America today, however, we have many Cub Scout dens that are not natural play groups. The boys may go to the same school, but the neighborhood idea may stretch in some cases to several miles.

While the Hickory Street boys spend a portion of their time in almost every yard in the neighborhood, for some reason most of their activity seems to take place in Eric's backyard. A game may start in another yard, but it doesn't take long for it to switch to Eric's. It's hard to know the reason for this, because all of the families have nice yards. Nevertheless, Eric's yard seems to be general headquarters. Since this is true, Eric's mother has for some time had the group on her hands.

Even the dogs of the community seem to have chosen Eric's yard for their hangout. When you add the dogs to the boys and put them all in one yard, you really have something. The problem becomes more acute when the boys get busy deciding what they will do. Especially when they decide upon the wrong things!

Eric's mother likes boys. Otherwise they would drive her frantic. But before Cub Scouting came to Hickory Street, her relationship to the boys was not very satisfactory. She had no basis

for helping the group in a positive way. Hers was a "no-no" type of leadership. It kept her busy just straightening out the arguments and keeping the boys out of serious trouble.

After Cub Scouting came to Hickory Street, no tremendous changes occurred. The gang that was already there merely became a den. You see, no one really organized the den on Hickory Street. It was there all the time, and the boys continue to make Eric's yard their headquarters. In other situations, the rural den or den from a school area may need more help to get started.

So the seven boys on Hickory Street became Den 4. It is likely that the dogs hardly noticed the change from the gang to den. But now, Eric's mother and the parents in the neighborhood discovered that things seemed to go more smoothly. There was a more natural basis for Eric's mother to work with boys. The fun went on as it had before, only there was more of it now and an opportunity for boys to taste the satisfaction of accomplishment and have fun at the same time.

What really happened, then, was that Cub Scouting merely recognized the natural play group which already existed on Hickory Street. Leadership and program were added, and everyone was happy with the result.

THE LEADERS OF DEN 4

THE DEN MOTHER.—Since Eric's mother had long had the boys on her hands, it was natural for her to continue that relationship as Den Mother. In a way she had been serving as Den Mother for a long time, only now it became official. Now she had the advantage of a definite program to follow and other leaders to work with her.

ASSISTANT DEN MOTHER.—Robby's mother was willing to help so she became the assistant Den Mother. An assistant is important, as she can share the work and is a made-to-order successor if the Den Mother leaves the den or is absent. She can help in many ways as a parent contact and recordkeeper, and with mail, local publicity, or other details of den operations.

THE DEN CHIEF.—Eric's mother needed more help to lead a group of active boys, so a Boy Scout was recruited as den chief when the old gang became Den 4.

As in Den 4, your den chief will be a Boy Scout. He probably belongs to the troop that is sponsored by the same institution that sponsors your pack; otherwise he will come from a nearby troop. The Cubmaster will work with the Scoutmaster to recruit your den chief.

Your den chief will help you and your den only to the extent that you develop a good relationship with him. You'll find out how he can help in chapter 18, "You and Your Den Chief."

THE DEN DAD.—There is a natural tendency on the part of dads to "let mother do it" when it comes to bringing up children. Dads find it convenient to leave a large share of that side of life to you. Confidentially, they wouldn't pass the buck to you so often if you didn't let them get away with it.

That is one of the reasons it is wise to add a dad who will serve as den dad. Often he is the Den Mother's husband, and Cub Scouting leadership becomes a family experience. That's why Eric's dad was chosen by the parents as den dad of Den 4.

The den dad's first responsibility is to represent the parents of the boys in the den. He is usually invited to serve as a member of the pack committee.

His second responsibility is to work with the fathers of the boys in his den. He interests them in their own boys as well as in Cub Scouting. He urges them to attend monthly pack meetings and assists in every way he can in showing them how to work with their boys on the achievement program.

The den dad cooperates with the Den Mother in securing special materials which may be necessary. He gets the other dads of the den to work on such special projects as helping the boys fix up the meeting place or build an outdoor den shelter.

From time to time the den dad arranges and leads a father-and-son outing. These are simple affairs and are held as often as may seem wise. An outing might be a wiener roast or ball game or nature ramble.

The den dad can be of great help to you at pack meetings. He assists in setting up exhibits, getting ready for den stunts, and making certain the parents are present to take part in their sons' advancement ceremonies.

So you see, by having a den dad in every den, we find it easier to get interest and help from fathers. Otherwise, they may be content merely to give the Den Mother a vote of confidence.

THE DENNER.—The boys of Den 4 elected Mike as denner. It was natural for them to select him, because he was oldest.

It is the denner's job to help the den chief whenever possible. He arrives early to help with last-minute preparations for the den meeting, and he remains after the den meeting to help put the meeting place back in order. Sometimes he will lead a song or act as cheerleader or assist in the leadership of the den.

The denner serves for an indefinite time. It is more satisfactory to make it a short period. This will give a number of the boys a chance to serve and will be more pleasing to the boys than to have one boy serve for a long time. The denner's two gold bars, worn on his left sleeve during his term, should be presented in a den or pack ceremony. These bars are worn as long as he is in office, then removed from his sleeve.

THE ASSISTANT DENNER.—Robby was elected assistant denner of Den 4. He would act as denner if Mike were absent. He keeps the den diary and reads it at the den meeting once a month. He, too, serves an indefinite term, and during that time wears a single gold bar on his left sleeve.

It is important that the members elect their denner and assistant. Cub Scout age is not too early to start American boys on democratic practices. The experience of deciding by vote and then living with their decision is valuable.

THE DEN ON YOUR STREET

It is to your advantage to see that your den does not grow beyond the number you can easily handle. Six or eight boys would normally be quite enough to keep you and your den chief busy during the weekly den meetings, but there is no rule about the size of dens. You and your pack leaders make this decision.

Once you have taken as many of the boys in your neighborhood into your den as you feel you can successfully lead, then it will be the responsibility of the Cubmaster and the pack committee to organize additional dens to take care of the other boys.

You may know the boys well and see them everyday, because they are friends of your own boy. You will have a pleasant relationship with their parents. You will have leaders to assist you in planning weekly den meeting programs. You will have a den chief to assist you in working with the boys. In the chapters to follow you will learn more about these things.

Some dens will be natural neighborhood groups, some may not. Some will be rural, some suburban, and some city. The material which follows can be adapted to any of these circumstances.

3. THE DEN MEETING PLACE

"Let's build a shack!"

That's been a watchword ever since boys were invented. Every boy wants a room of his own at home. Every group of boys wants some sort of hangout that it can call its own. It's one of those natural urges which you just can't knock out of boys' heads.

If you deny them the privilege of a home base, it's likely that they'll go out and develop one of their own, perhaps an undesirable one. So it's much better that you have a part in helping them to satisfy this urge than attempt to smother it.

You can see how important it is for the den to have a somewhat permanent place in which to meet. If the boys meet in a different place every week or every month, they do not feel they have a home. Much of the value of the den idea is lost when it becomes necessary for the boys to shift about in their meeting places.

That means that a Den Mother should serve as long as she possibly can. Each time a new Den Mother takes over, the boys must adjust to a new personality and to a new den home.

Ideally, the boys should have a place that they can fix up a bit. Of course, all dens do not have such facilities. There are many situations where no family in the entire den will have an ideal place in which the den can meet. However, even though they may have to meet in a kitchen or living room, it is best that they meet in the same house as long as possible. In this way the surroundings become familiar and they feel more at home. They learn to take care of the furniture and to do whatever else may be necessary to fit themselves into the location.

Pride in "ownership" is a strong stimulus for keeping a neat home or meeting place; and if the Cub Scouts are made to feel that the den meeting place is really theirs one afternoon a week, they will take good care of it.

MAKE THE BEST OF WHAT YOU HAVE

Many American homes have no large recreation rooms or space in basements or attics which can easily be used for den meetings. Most homes have little unused space. That means you simply have to make the best of it.

Most dens across the country meet in the Den Mother's kitchen, basement, or living room. Many dens meet in apartment houses. Whatever your situation, it should encourage you to know that many mothers are holding successful den meetings under conditions like yours.

If you must hold your den meetings in your living room, try to anticipate possible accidents. If you do this, the chances are you can avoid most of them.

For example, rather than leaving that fragile lamp on the living room table and attempting to keep the Cub Scouts away from it, move the lamp to the dining room on den meeting day. If you have a beautiful but not very sturdy antique chair, don't expect the boys to treat it respectfully. As you know, boys do not just sit on chairs; they are inclined to fall into them, so take that beautiful Victorian chair to the dining room, too. That's the best way to guarantee that it won't be broken, and it will protect your peace of mind.

If there is a section of your living room containing things which you do not want the boys to handle, then get the den dad to help you find or make some inexpensive folding screens which can be used to partition off that portion. These can be decorated and used as bulletin boards.

Instead of having your boys sit on your davenport, give them a chance to make some seats or stools of their own. It's a fine father-and-son project. These, too, may be put away after every meeting. It will help to give the boys the feeling that they have their own place.

TYPES OF MEETING PLACES

Without knowing your home, we can't very well tell you the best place to hold a den meeting, but we can give you some samples of places that have been used.

Since most dens meet in some room in the home that is used for other purposes, this is probably your situation. But first look around to make certain that you are not overlooking some practical place that might be adapted for Cub Scout use.

For example, during many months of the year perhaps your den could meet in your garage. All you need to do is back out the car and have the boys get out their homemade furniture, den doodle, and bulletin board. In some sections of the country this would be a fine meeting place all year.

If you have a large yard, perhaps the fathers can help you to build a combination den hut and toolhouse. It's the rare situation indeed in which the den must meet inside the house year-round. The boys will want to meet outdoors during the spring, summer, and fall, whenever possible.

If you live in an apartment house, see whether the management will let you use a small storeroom or basement hall, or maybe there is a place on the roof. If that isn't possible, plan your den meetings to fit your apartment. Use crafts and games that do not require running. Move outside for active games to the garage or driveway.

Remember, there are hundreds of dens in our largest cities successfully meeting in apartments. If their Den Mothers can do it, surely you can too.

HOW ABOUT THE BASEMENT?

Don't overlook the basement even though it may not look very appealing at the moment. Use your imagination. Try to figure out what might be done with a little energy and imagination. You need not spend your own energy. Ask the den dad to call upon the fathers of the den to work with the boys in helping to clean up and paint a corner of your basement that you are willing to turn over to the boys. Let them furnish not only the energy to do the work but the paint and material, too. Mothers will enjoy adding the woman's touch to this cleaning and decorating bee for the den meeting place.

You will find most parents will help in this way if you'll just make clear the sort of help you need. They realize the contribution you are making, and they'll welcome a chance to help. However, you can't expect help, if you do not ask for it.

PART II
YOUR DEN MEETING

4. HOW TO RUN IT

Did you ever play bounce ball? It's a good den game—one which your boys will enjoy. All you need is a rubber ball and a wastebasket. Place the basket on the ground. Line up the boys in front of it. Each boy tries to bounce the ball and make it land in the basket. No matter how well he bounces the ball, he does not score unless it lands in the basket on the first bounce.

In a way, your den meetings are like bounce ball. No matter how fine a time boys have *in* the den meetings, they do not get full value unless there is a bounce carrying over from the den meetings into the other days of the week. In other words, you plan your den meetings in such a way that boys get ideas for things to do at home—it's the carryover that really counts.

HOW LONG SHOULD YOUR MEETING LAST?

It's a lot better to have a short meeting and keep it moving than to have a longer one and let it drag. It's better to send the boys away wishing the meeting had been longer than to keep them so long they wish it would end.

Most den meetings do not last longer than 1 or 1¼ hours. If this seems short, remember the bounce idea. All of a boy's Cub Scouting does not happen in the den meeting.

It's a good sign if, when the den meeting is over, the boys want to remain and do some more. If they have not finished something they are working on, perhaps that will encourage them to work on it at home and with each other during the week.

This is Cub Scouting as it should be, going on all the time and not just during den meetings. If the Cub Scout has something interesting to work on at home between meetings with his parents, then he is almost certain to be eager for the next den meeting so that he can show you the work he has done with his dad.

So plan for a fast-moving, intensive, 1-hour den meeting and send the boys away as soon as the meeting is over. Boys are fickle, and too much of even a good thing begins to pall after awhile.

DISCIPLINE PROBLEMS

Do you sometimes talk to other Den Mothers and the Den Leader coach about their dens? If so, does the problem of discipline ever creep into your conversation? Or are your boys always well behaved? Chances are once in a while you do experience what you consider a discipline problem.

A discipline problem is what happens when boys become less interested in what you try to get them to do than they are in what they can think up by themselves. In other words, if your boys get more satisfaction from kicking each other in the shins than from doing what you want them to—well, then they will probably kick each other in the shins.

Remember, you are having a contest with a group of boys during every meeting. If they learn that they can have more fun doing the things you bring them, then they'll probably do those things. If they look upon the den program as an interference with their fun, then you face a serious problem.

More often than not, then, a discipline problem is a *program* problem. A den meeting program which has been carefully planned to hold the interest of boys is not likely to require disciplinary measures.

LETTING OFF STEAM

A steam boiler has its safety valve. Steam pressure can build up just so far. Then it must be released through a safety valve or through an explosion. Boys are much like steam boilers. The pressure can build up just so far, then it must be released.

If you accept this as a simple fact, you will run your den meeting in such a way that boys are frequently given an opportunity to let off steam. They can sit still for only a very short time. When they have reached that limit something will happen, and that something is not likely to improve your disposition. So don't expect them to sit still and be quiet for long. Alternate "sitting" with "doing"; "quiet" with "less quiet."

CONTROL AND BALANCE

It's important to remember that you must keep your boys under control at all times. If you lose control of the group, it's most difficult to regain it. Yet, your controlling hand must not lie so heavily that your boys constantly feel smothered and held down.

Balance is the important thing. An atmosphere of spontaneous fun is necessary. You can have that and still keep the group under control. Go at it lightly, with a smile and with enthusiasm. Your boys will be flattered if they believe you, too, are having fun.

GETTING ATTENTION

If you lose control of the group, how can you regain it?

You might try to outshout your boys, but that isn't recommended. It ends with hoarseness and usually failure. The best way to get the attention of your boys is to stand where they can see you and raise your arm in the Cub Scout sign. (See page 126 for the Cub Scout sign.)

When they see you give this signal, they are to stop talking and raise their own arms in the sign. After you have used this signal a number of times, it will work. In the beginning, compliment the boy who returns your sign first. Next time you use the signal, the response will improve.

One last point about getting attention. Never try to get it by talking loudly. Talk very quietly, so the boys have to listen carefully to hear. This works best if the expression on your face indicates that you want to tell them something special. It also helps to have something interesting in your hands to show them.

THAT PROBLEM BOY

There is at least one problem boy in every den. Sometimes he is a problem because he is too vocal. Sometimes it's because he does things more quickly, and therefore he has a shorter interest span. Again it may be because he has more energy than you have been able to harness. Sometimes—but not often—that problem boy may be a boy whom nobody has found the answer to yet.

If you have a boy in your den who seems to be a problem, watch him carefully. Try to discover at what point he usually becomes a problem. Is it while you are leading the den? Or is it while the den chief is in charge? When this boy leads off in the other direction, do the others follow him?

There is no general remedy for you to use with all problem boys. Each requires different treatment.

There is one simple remedy which often works. If the problem boy tends to carry the others with him, then recognize such ability and give him a definite job. Perhaps you can work things out so that he can be elected the denner or the assistant denner.

Perhaps he accomplishes so little in the den that there is little basis for recognition or compliments. Such a boy usually has some special interests. Try to find out what they are. If he is loud, make him cheerleader. If he is musical, make him a song leader. If he is interested in bugs or animals, put him in charge of the den museum. If he is interested in baseball players, interest him in developing his own "Hall of Fame" pictures of the well-known players. Find some key interest and encourage him to follow it. Then be sure to recognize his accomplishments.

DEN MEETING ATTENDANCE

The attendance problem is much like the discipline problem. If the show is good, the boys will probably come. If there is a better show somewhere else, they will probably go to it.

It's a good idea to watch your community and try to discover what the boys are doing when they don't *have* to do anything. That may give you some valuable tips as to how you can make your den meetings more desirable.

For example, there are seasons of the year when certain sports demand a great deal of attention from all boys. You can even play baseball, but to do so you have to understand some of the reasons why such games are popular with boys. Boys like baseball because it combines competition with lots of action.

During the baseball season, therefore, you will want to use various types of baseball games. They are rugged and competitive and help teach Cub Scouts how to bat and catch a ball. Several kinds of baseball games are described in the Wolf and Bear books. You can use them in your meetings. There will be times, too, when your den may enjoy a game with another den in a nearby park.

If you would have good attendance at your den meetings, then, have a good program. It is just about as simple as that. There isn't any other factor that can make up for the lack of a good program.

Of course, there are other attendance factors, too, such as the attitude of the parents. Still another factor is the den meeting place. Boys are not likely to be happy meeting indoors in the balmy spring and summer months. So move into the open. However, if it is very hot someday, you will be surprised at the enthusiasm the boys will show for a meeting in their usual place in the basement.

5. A TYPICAL MEETING

A good working pattern for the den meeting has been developed through long experience. You would do well to follow this pattern, at least until you are well grounded in Cub Scouting and feel confident enough to vary it.

The pattern divides the den meetings into seven parts. Each has a purpose, and, if you use them regularly, you will find that every meeting will have the essentials. Here are the *seven parts:*

1. BEFORE THE MEETING STARTS
2. WHILE CUB SCOUTS GATHER
3. OPENING
4. BUSINESS ITEMS
5. ACTIVITIES
6. CLOSING
7. AFTER THE MEETING

Now let's go through a typical meeting, explaining what happens during each part.

PART 1—BEFORE THE MEETING STARTS

Sometimes it is difficult for the den chief to arrive at the meeting ahead of the boys. His school may let out later. If this is true, you just have to make the best of it until he can arrive. Plan your program so the games and activities led by the den chief are scheduled after he is sure to be there.

If your den chief can arrive ahead of the boys, it gives you a fine opportunity to sit down with him and make sure everything is set for the meeting. Try to get the denner to arrive a little earlier, too, so he can be sure that the meeting place is ready.

The purpose of the "before the meeting starts" part is to give you and your assistant Den Mother a chance to make whatever last-minute preparations are necessary for your program.

PART 2—WHILE CUB SCOUTS GATHER

Boys rarely have great trouble deciding on something to do. The trouble comes after they decide. They have the faculty for filling every empty moment with something that may be a little less desirable than what you might wish them to do. The moral is —don't leave too many empty moments.

As soon as the first boy arrives at your door, give him something to do. Get him started on the gathering-time project before he has time to think of anything else. Don't wait until he gets inside and prepares to scuffle with another boy.

For example, if it is Things That Fly month, the den chief (or you) meets each boy at the door with two pieces of paper.

"Hi, Charley," says the den chief. "Hang up your hat and coat right away, because we're going to have a paper airplane contest right in the beginning of the den meeting. Make two of them with these two pieces of paper and practice with them to see if you can win the contest."

That isn't foolproof, but it helps. If you don't plan to fill this period (with guided activity) while the boys are arriving, they will fill it with roughhousing. Just anticipate what boys will do under certain circumstances, then arrange the circumstances to be sure that they do the best thing. They will have more fun, and so will you. The *Cub Scout Magic* book* has ideas you can use.

Some Den Mothers find it is convenient to check up on the boys' achievements during the gathering time. It is also a good time for the Den Mother to collect dues.

PART 3—OPENING

The opening serves notice on the boys that the meeting is really starting. It follows the gathering period, which was informal and without much organization. A good opening period provides a natural transition to the more organized activities of the meeting.

OPENING CEREMONY.—Boys like to make noise and to do things together. Try combining those two things in the opening period and give them a chance to make noise together. This can include a song, a yell, a rhythmic applause stunt, or something which gives them a chance to let off steam. This can be led by the den chief. Use suggestions from your *Scouting Magazine* and

---

To order *Cub Scout Magic* and the other publications and forms mentioned throughout this book, use the catalog numbers listed in chapter 23, "Helps for You."

Cub Scout Program Helps. You'll also find some good opening ceremonies in the next chapter of this book.

ROLL CALL.—While a roll call isn't necessary, boys enjoy responding to their names in some unique way. Sometimes you can relate the roll call to the theme of the month. For example, if it's Nature month, ask them to respond with the name of a bird, animal, or tree. Let the denner call the roll.

UNIFORM CHECKUP.—Occasionally it is a good idea to have a uniform inspection during the opening period. Check the boys' uniforms to be sure they are worn properly. Don't be too severe; remember that you are dealing with boys. This can be a good assignment for the den chief.

PART 4—BUSINESS ITEMS

Usually you will not have much business to conduct in your den meetings. It is best to keep them informal.

If you do not collect the dues and check the boys' books for achievements during the gathering time, you can do it during the main part of the meeting. Also cover anything else that you may have in the way of decisions to be made.

Especially during the first den meeting of the month, you have a lot of plans to make regarding the month's theme, which is the same for all Cub Scout dens in your pack. (See chapter 13, "Your Program—Who Plans It," for an explanation of themes.) Discuss the way in which your den will fit into the theme. Also decide what the den will do at the pack meeting.

Have you ever tried to eat a Dagwood sandwich? Confidentially, they're a mess. Imagine one like this if you can.

Start with four slices of bread all together with nothing between them. Then comes a thick slice of Bermuda onion. Cover it with something sticky like peanut butter so that the slice of tomato which you're going to put on next will stay put. Then add whatever you can find until it won't stand up any more. Then it's a completed Dagwood sandwich.

Can you imagine trying to eat a sandwich like that? It would be far too large to put in your mouth, and the bread wouldn't come in the right places. It wouldn't be very appetizing.

Den meetings are somewhat like sandwiches. They are either the Dagwood type or the club type. In the Dagwood type you can put all of the business or "sit and take it" parts of the meeting in one place and all of the "get up and do it" parts of the meeting in another. That's no more appetizing than the Dagwood sandwich.

Boys are able to sit still just so long—no longer. The important thing is to give them opportunities to let off steam.

So build your den meetings like club sandwiches. Start with a layer of activity, then put in a layer of "sit and take it," but slice this part thin. Alternate the quiet portions of the meeting with the active portions, because, if you try to have too much quiet, it won't be quiet anyway.

In order to differentiate between the business parts of the meeting and the activities parts, we list them separately. In the development of your den meeting program you will probably find it wiser to alternate one with the other.

PART 5—ACTIVITIES

GAMES.—Include at least one game, and preferably two, in every den meeting. You'll have to choose whatever games fit your meeting place. There are many fine quiet ones that do not require much space. However, if your meeting place does not permit the lively type, get away once in a while to a local park so the boys can have more action. You'll find both your denner and den chief a great help to you in the leadership of games. Usually, it works best if your den chief leads the games, but does not play in them.

You'll find some games in chapter 8 of this book and about 500 in *Games for Cub Scouts*.

CRAFTS.—Don't overdo on crafts. Avoid busy work and those cut and paste projects. It isn't necessary for boys to complete their craft projects in the meetings. Give them patterns, get them started, and get them interested enough during the meeting *so they will take their unfinished projects home and work on them with their dads.* Crafts should be the outcome of a program theme.

Since you have more patience than the den chief, your craft program will be more effective if you lead it. Of course, get the den chief to help. (See chapter 9 for more on crafts.)

TRICKS AND PUZZLES.—These are among the trademarks of Cub Scouting. They have an appeal for every boy. The tricks should not be complicated. Each boy may take a turn bringing a trick, which he finds with the help of his dad. First he tries to fool the den, then he teaches it to the other boys, and they in turn go home and use it on their dads.

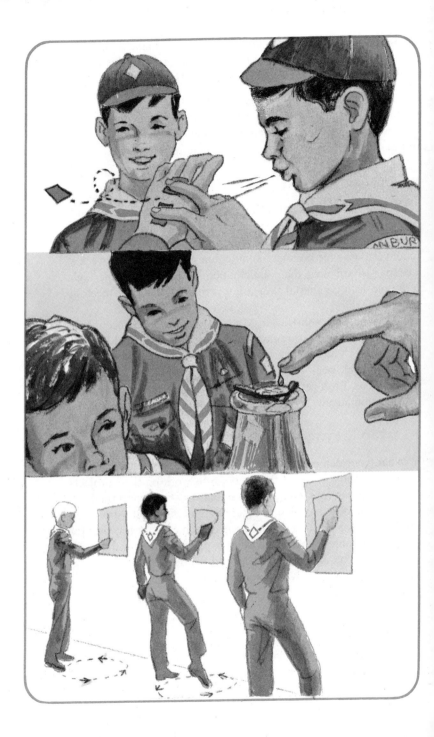

Puzzles should be of the type that boys can make as a craft project. You will find more on these in chapter 11 of this book, the *Den Chief's Denbook,* and *Cub Scout Magic.*

PREPARATIONS FOR THE PACK MEETING.—At den meetings during the month, the boys rehearse their den stunts, put finishing touches on their costumes that are used occasionally, and make plans for exhibits—aimed at the pack meeting.

PART 6—CLOSING

Usually the closing period of the meeting is more quiet and serious in tone than the opening. It's a fine time for the Den Mother to present a very short closing thought. In addition, she should also give the boys last-minute reminders about next week's meeting—sharpening their anticipation by mentioning the high spot, and listing material they are to bring for the pack meeting stunt and exhibit.

Following this short Den Mother's minute, the meeting is usually closed with a ceremony. Den ceremonies should be kept simple and should be varied from meeting to meeting. Mere repetition each week of the Cub Scout Promise tends to become monotonous. Boys get to the point where they merely repeat these words automatically.

PART 7—AFTER THE MEETING

When your den meeting is over, it's a good idea to see that the boys go directly home. If they stay on to work on their projects or play around your home, parents may become concerned.

When the boys have left, the denner remains to help straighten up the meeting place. You and your den chief work together for just a few minutes. You review what happened and how the meeting plan can be improved. At the end of the third den meeting, you fill out the Den Advancement Report.

GETTING THE THEME STARTED IN THE DEN

The first den meeting of each month is the most important. That's when you get across to the boys the theme for your whole month of Cub Scouting. If the boys become interested in the theme, you'll probably have a highly successful month.

It might be easy for you to organize your den program by assigning certain theme projects to each boy. However, you'll hardly find this the most effective way for interesting boys in the theme of the month.

You'll find boys will become interested in the theme if you ask them leading questions about what they would like to do, rather than tell them what you would like them to do. If you ask the right questions, the den usually winds up doing the things that you would have suggested to them anyway.

For example, let's say it's the first meeting of the month in which your pack is using the Indian theme. You could launch the theme by telling the boys that during the first week everyone will make an Indian headdress, the second week a pair of moccasins, the third week an Indian shield, and the fourth week a tomahawk. But that would be regimentation, wouldn't it? Even though these projects might be perfectly natural things for boys to do, the fact that you are telling the boys to do them lessens their appeal.

Now let's take a different tack. Suppose you open the discussion about the Indian theme by a leading question: "How many of you boys wish you might have been real Indians?"

Of course, most boys would like to be Indians in the days of the pioneers. (Incidentally, some Cub Scouts *are* Indians.)

"If we can't be real Indians, we can still have a lot of fun doing some of the things Indians did. Suppose you were going to start being Indians tomorrow. What are some of the things you would have to do?"

"The first thing we would have to do," says Billy, "is to dress like Indians. We have to have an Indian headdress."

"Sure enough, Bill. Would you *make* one of the big feather headdresses, or would you make a small one?"

"Well, I haven't got enough feathers for a big headdress, but I saw a picture of one where you only need three or four feathers. I think I could make that one."

"What else would you have to do if you were going to start being Indians?"

"We would have to make a tomahawk," says Jimmy.

"Well, I suppose you would make one out of stone, wouldn't you, Jimmy?" you ask.

"Gee, no," answers Jimmy. "That would be too hard. I think I could make one out of wood, though."

"Say, that's a good idea. Well, what else now? You couldn't be an Indian just by having a headdress and a tomahawk."

"I 'spect we would have to have bows and arrows," says Fred.

"Why yes, most Indians did have bows and arrows," you answer. "They cost a lot of money, though."

"Not the kind I make," answered Fred. "I can make one out of a willow branch and a piece of string. That's the kind I make."

On the conversation and the questions go, until the first thing the boys know they have planned what they would like to do during Indian month. And it was all done by a few carefully worded questions from the Den Mother. The boys thought up the ideas, and they are those which most appealed to them. Try this method and you'll become so skillful with it that it will usually work.

IDEAS FOR DEN MEETINGS

The place to plan your den meetings for the month is the monthly pack leaders' meeting. There you will work together with the Cubmaster, Den Leader coach, and other Den Mothers to develop den meeting outlines for the following month.

Den meetings are planned around specific themes. Therefore, the things you choose for your den meeting programs depend a great deal upon the theme your pack has adopted for the month.

Cub Scout Program Helps are inserted in segments in *Scouting Magazine,* which is sent to all den and pack leaders. They are also produced as an annual, available as a sales item. The segments contain ideas for suggested themes during the months ahead.

Understanding the den meeting pattern discussed in this chapter, you are able to work with the Den Leader coach and the other Den Mothers during your monthly meeting to plan specific den meetings. If your pack doesn't have a Den Leader coach, this planning is done at the monthly pack leaders' meeting.

ONE MONTH'S DEN MEETINGS

To help you see more clearly how the den activities for a month are related to a theme, here is a typical month of activity in a den. In this case, the meetings are built around the Cub Scout Handymen theme. Outlines for the meetings are planned at the monthly meeting with the Den Leader coach or at the pack leaders' meetings, which are attended by all adult pack leaders, including Den Mothers.

The various activities for the Handymen theme are described below so that you may better understand the projects referred to in the den meetings.

HOME INSPECTION.—Boys and dads inspect homes in search of repair jobs.

HOMEMADE GADGETS.—Dads and sons make homemade gadgets, such as broom holders, knife racks, shoescrapers, and shoe racks.

HELP THE DEN MOTHER.—The den dad and the Cub Scouts select some project which needs to be done around the home of the Den Mother.

THE CUB SCOUT'S ROOM.—Boys plan ways of fixing up their rooms or something around the house and carry out their plans during the month. Mother and dad will help with this project, of course.

NAIL-DRIVING CONTEST.—Each den picks its champion. Then the den champions hammer away to select the pack champion at the pack meeting.

PACK MEETING EXHIBIT.—Each den exhibits its homemade gadgets, dad-and-son repair jobs, and things Cub Scouts made for their rooms.

Now with these suggestions in mind, let's turn and see how they work in the four weekly den meetings during Handymen month.

DEN MEETING 1

BEFORE THE MEETING STARTS.—If the den chief is able to arrive a few moments early, he and the Den Mother and the assistant Den Mother check on last-minute details. The denner also arrives early to prepare the meeting place.

WHILE CUB SCOUTS GATHER.—As the boys arrive, the den chief teaches them how to set and drive a nail.

OPENING.—Have the Cub Scouts form in a hollow square and sing a song from the *Cub Scout Songbook*.

BUSINESS ITEMS.—Den Mother explains the Handymen theme. She checks on the achievements passed since the last den meeting and collects dues. She explains home inspection projects, urging the boys to start the next day. She discusses homemade gadgets with the boys, showing pictures and ideas. Each boy chooses a gadget he will start at home with his dad.

ACTIVITIES.—The den chief helps boys practice for the nail-driving contest and explains how it fits into the pack meeting. Play one of the games described in chapter 8 or the *Cub Scout Program Helps*. Teach boys blow-hard trick, as follows:

Place three small bits of paper on the back of your hand. Let anyone select one of the pieces. You claim that you can control your breath so as to blow away only the selected bit. This seems impossible, but there is a catch to it. Place two fingers of your other hand on the other bits of paper and blow the selected one.

CLOSING.—Remind the boys to complete their home projects before the next meeting when they will report on repairs they are doing with their dads. Suggest they practice nail driving. Have the boys form a circle and repeat the Cub Scout Promise.

AFTER THE MEETING.—The Den Mother meets briefly with the den chief to review the meeting. The denner straightens up the meeting room.

DEN MEETING 2

BEFORE THE MEETING STARTS. The Den Mother, assistant Den Mother, and den chief meet to check on last-minute details of the program, The denner prepares for the den meeting.

WHILE CUB SCOUTS GATHER.—As the boys arrive, the den chief shows how to drill and countersink a hole for a screw.

OPENING.—The Den Mother calls the roll, and each boy answers by showing the gadget he started at home.

BUSINESS ITEMS.—The boys report on the home inspection project, mentioning repair jobs they have started with their dads. The Den Mother checks on achievements and collects dues. She shows magazine clippings or tells about simple ideas for fixing up boys' rooms. The Den Mother leaves the room while the den chief discusses with boys possible help-the-Den-Mother projects. (Between this den meeting and the next, the den chief will have phoned the den dad for ideas and help on this.)

ACTIVITIES.—Repeat the nail-driving contest. Announce that the den champion will be chosen at the last den meeting. Play a game, or teach boys a magic dime trick as follows:

Break a wooden match halfway through, being careful not to break it entirely. Lay it across the top of a milk bottle and put a dime on top of it. Ask someone if he can make the dime fall into the bottle without touching the coin, match, or bottle. To do it, simply let a drop or two of water fall on the broken end of the match. This causes the match to straighten out and the dime then falls into the bottle.

CLOSING.—Explain more den handymen contests. Form a circle around the flag, and sing "America."

AFTER THE MEETING.—The den chief and Den Mother meet briefly to review the meeting. The denner straightens up the room.

DEN MEETING 3

BEFORE THE MEETING STARTS.—The den chief arrives early to go over the program with the Den Mother and the assistant Den Mother for a last-minute checkup. The denner prepares the meeting place.

WHILE CUB SCOUTS GATHER.—As boys arrive, the den chief demonstrates and has each Cub Scout make a sanding block padded with sponge rubber under the sandpaper.

OPENING.—The den chief teaches the boys a new yell.

BUSINESS ITEMS.—Den Mother checks achievements and collects dues. Determine which home-repair project each boy will demonstrate with his dad at the pack meeting. (Have each boy write his dad a note regarding this.) Plan homemade exhibits.

ACTIVITIES.—Help boys with partially finished homemade gadgets so that they may bring them to the pack meeting. Conduct countersinking and screwdriving contest. Announce that a den champion nail-driver will be selected at the next meeting. Boys show gadgets they are making for their rooms. Teach try-your-coordination stunt as follows:

Each boy tries to print a B on a large piece of paper while standing on his left foot and swinging his right foot in a circle.

CLOSING.—Remind boys that den champion nail-drivers and screw-drivers will be selected next meeting. Have boys bring to the next den meeting all homemade gadgets and items made for their rooms. Form a living circle (explained on page 127). Then say, "Do your best." The boys answer, "We'll do our best."

AFTER THE MEETING.—The Den Mother and den chief meet briefly to fill out the Den Advancement Report for the Cubmaster. Then Den Mother or Den Leader coach gives this to the Cubmaster at the pack leaders' meeting in time to get awards for the pack meeting. The denner straightens up the room.

DEN MEETING 4

BEFORE THE MEETING.—The Den Mother, the assistant Den Mother, and den chief check on last-minute details of the program while the denner prepares the den meeting place.

WHILE CUB SCOUTS GATHER.—Practice nail-driving contest preparatory to den contest.

OPENING.—Boys give the pledge of allegiance to the flag.

BUSINESS ITEMS.—Eliminate this business meeting.

ACTIVITIES.—Conduct the den champion nail-driving contest and select the den champion. Help boys with finishing touches on the gadgets. Teach "betcha" trick as follows: Betcha can't fold a piece of paper in half more than nine times. It can't be done. Use an 8½- by 11-inch sheet first. Then try one page of newspaper.

CLOSING.—Urge boys to get parents to attend the pack meeting. If time permits, have each boy write a note to take home to parents. Remind them to bring exhibit material to pack meeting as well as material they will need to demonstrate their home jobs. Sing a quiet song.

AFTER THE MEETING.—Den Mother and den chief meet briefly to review meeting. Denner straightens up room.

HANDYMEN AT THE PACK MEETING

All of this activity on the Handymen theme finally is climaxed at the monthly meeting of the pack. Your den would have a table to display the gadgets made at home and at the four den meetings. Your den champion in nail driving would compete against the best from the other Cub Scout dens.

Many times your den will prepare a skit or a stunt based on the theme. For full details on pack meetings, see chapter 12.

6. CEREMONIES

Why ceremonies, anyway?

W ell, watch your Cub Scouts when a craft project is completed, a race is won, or a game is over, and notice how pleased they are when you compliment them for a job well done. Well-executed ceremonies can bring even greater joy to a Cub Scout because they give him recognition.

The Cub Scout is at an age when ceremonies can be used to get across the Cub Scout ideals. For this reason, they are used frequently in both the den and the pack. The pack ceremonies, which are usually under the leadership of the Cubmaster, are more elaborate than those you will use. Keep yours simple, short, and suited to the occasion.

You can use simple ceremonies in opening and closing the den meeting and to mark important events in the lives of your Cub Scouts and the whole den.

If recognition comes naturally and at frequent intervals, boys will not be tempted to seek recognition in less-desirable ways. If the boy does not achieve recognition naturally, then he may very well become a problem in the den as he seeks to attract attention.

The Den Mother, therefore, should seek opportunities to recognize boys in informal ceremonies throughout the year.

Here are four things to remember in planning den ceremonies.

♦ Keep Them Simple

Simplicity is important in den ceremonies. If you make them too elaborate, the pack meeting ceremonies may seem less important. Don't bother with written parts and don't get involved with much ritual.

You will keep your den ceremonies simple if, occasionally, you give the boys an opportunity to plan and lead them. This gives the boys experience and also helps them meet the ceremony requirement of the Flag achievement for Wolf Cub Scouts. En-

courage the boys to use their imaginations and develop new ceremonies rather than merely repeat the same old ones. When a boy is going to lead the ceremony, have him tell you a week in advance what he is going to do. If you don't, you may get a surprise for which you are not prepared.

♦ Keep Them Short

One or two minutes should be long enough for any den ceremony. After all, you are only marking within the den certain occasions that will often be recognized at the pack meeting.

♦ Relate Them to Everyday Experiences

Build your den ceremonies around everyday experiences of the boy and the den.

♦ Don't Get in a Rut

Vary your ceremonies so that boys do not tire of them. Don't open the den meeting and close it in the same way each week. Since den ceremonies are simple, it should not be difficult to have a great variety of them. Boys like something new.

OPENING CEREMONIES

As a general rule, you'll want to get your den meetings off to a rousing start with an opening ceremony that gives the boys a chance to work off steam. It will tend to bring them together after the less-organized activity while they have been gathering.

Here are some suggestions for your opening ceremonies:

1. A Cub Scout song (see the next chapter).
2. The den yell if your den has one.
3. Applause stunts. Boys clap in unison to rhythm such as 1, 2, 3, 4; 1, 2, 1, 2; 1, 2, 3, 4; 1, 2, 1, 2; 1, 2, 3, 4; 1, 2, 3, 4; 1.

   Applause stunts can be worked out in many different ways such as clapping to the tune of a lively song.

   Echo applause. Boys form two lines facing each other. One side claps 1, 2, 3, 4; the other side answers 1, 2, 1, 2; etc.
4. Form the boys in a circle and pass the Cub Scout handshake from one to the other. (See page 126 for the handshake.)
5. Form a hollow square and sing a song.
6. The den chief calls the roll. As each Cub Scout's name is called, he comes forward and gives the den chief the Cub Scout handshake.

7. The grand howl (short version). Cub Scouts form a circle. Each boy squats, touching the fingers of both hands to the ground between the feet. Then, like wolves, the Cub Scouts raise their heads and give a long howl, "Ah-h—kay-y—la! We-e-e'll do-o-o ou-u-r best!" As the last word—best—is yelled very sharply, everyone jumps to his feet, raises his hands high above his head, and gives the Cub Scout sign. (See page 126 for the sign.)

8. Special roll call. This might consist of having each boy answer with something related to the month's theme. It might be to name a bird or tree, show and explain something he has made since the last den meeting, name his favorite book or hobby, or tell his mother's first name.

9. Christmas opening. You or the den chief points out that the gifts we receive should make us more determined to live up to the ideals of Cub Scouting—duty to God and to our fellowman. After repeating the pledge of allegiance and the Law of the Pack, sing a Christmas carol and "Jingle Bells."

10. Mob scene. This is a yell done in parts like a round. Divide the den into four groups, and then have each repeat three times, "Fire! Fire!—Water! Water!—Help! Help!—Save my child!" (Two-beat rhythm will keep groups together.)

11. A prayer. Choose one suitable for all faiths unless all boys are members of the same faith.

12. Inspection of uniforms and for personal neatness.

13. Brief remarks about a famous man such as Washington; Lincoln; George Washington Carver; or Lord Baden-Powell, the founder of Scouting.

14. A reading such as Lincoln's "Gettysburg Address."

15. Candle ceremony. For this you need one small candle and one big one. Ask the Cub Scouts to close their eyes.
DEN MOTHER: Think about darkness.
DEN CHIEF: Now open your eyes. I will light this tiny candle. *(Lights candle.)* This small ray of light represents the goodwill given by one Cub Scout. See how it shines. Just as the rays from several candles can make a bright light, so can the goodwill of several Cub Scouts create much happiness.
DEN MOTHER: I now light this tall candle. *(Light it.)* Over all there shines a brighter light to lead us. Let us always think first of God; second, of others; and third, of ourselves.

GRAND HOWL

The grand howl is a ceremony that combines showing respect for a leader with a chance to use up energy. It serves equally well as an opening or closing ceremony for a den or pack. It's especially good outdoors.

The Cub Scouts stand in a circle. When a person is being honored, he or she stands in the center. Starting from a crouching position, the boys make the two-finger Cub Scout sign; but instead of putting their right arms over their heads, they touch the ground between their feet with the two fingers of both hands. Then, wolf-like, the Cub Scouts raise their heads and howl, "Ah-h—kay-y—la! We-e-e'll do-o-o ou-u-r best!" The last word "best" is yelled in unison. As it is yelled, the Cub Scouts jump to their feet, with both hands high above their heads in the Cub Scout sign.

The hands are held high while the denner or den chief calls to the Cub Scouts at the top of his voice, "dyb-dyb-dyb-dyb," meaning Do Your Best. On the fourth "dyb," each Cub Scout drops his left hand smartly to his side, makes the Cub Scout salute with his right, and shouts, "We-e-e'll dob-dob-dob-dob," meaning "We'll do our best." After the fourth "dob," each Cub Scout drops his right hand smartly to his side and comes to attention.

PATRIOTIC CEREMONIES

As part of every den meeting, include a song or ceremony that will help your Cub Scouts to understand better the flag, our country, or the meaning of Cub Scout citizenship. Use the Wolf and Bear Cub Scout books for ideas on these ceremonies.

◆ Have boys give the Cub Scout salute and repeat the pledge of allegiance to the flag.

◆ Plan a ceremony on the history of the flag. Each boy can make and color a different paper flag to show how our present flag was formed.

◆ Boys can put on ceremony based on a historic person whose birthday is during the month of the den meeting. For example, Abraham Lincoln or George Washington for February.

◆ Read and have den act out a simple story about one of our famous persons.

♦ Have Cub Scouts march past American flag or the den flag or both saluting. Place the American flag on right, of course.

♦ Parade the American flag and den flag past line of Cub Scouts who stand at attention and salute.

♦ My flag. A week before this ceremony is to be used, ask each Cub Scout to prepare and bring to the next den meeting a short statement on "What My Flag Means to Me." Select an interesting one and ask the writer to read it.

♦ This old flag. All read the verse as the flag is held aloft.

This old flag is my protection,
This old flag is my birthright,
This old flag is full of beauty.
May it fly both day and night,
It's an honor to salute it,
And with pride we hold it high,
We will keep it flying o'er us,
Like a symbol in the sky.

BIRTHDAY CEREMONIES

The Individual Cub Scout Record gives you the birthday of each of your Cub Scouts. Check these records for birthdays.

1. When a boy has a birthday, call him in front of the den during the opening of the meeting. You can recognize him in many different ways. You can sing "Happy Birthday" or give him a yell. You can present him with a simple birthday card, perhaps one made by the rest of the boys. You might light candles, one for each year. As each boy lights a candle, let him say something to the boy whose birthday it is.

2. The Cub Scout whose birthday is being recognized stands at a table with the other Cub Scouts. The denner enters with a birthday cake with lighted candles and places the cake in front of the honored Cub Scout. The den sings "Happy Birthday," and the Cub Scout makes a wish and blows out the candles. The boy standing at his right then claps once, the next boy twice, and so on until the age of the Cub Scout is

reached. Then all applaud. The boy's mother usually is happy to be asked to furnish the cake.

3. This is a ceremony for a boy who has reached his ninth birthday and is ready to start on the Bear Cub Scout achievements. You need a cake, candles, and a *Bear Cub Scout Book.*

DENNER: *(Name)* had his ninth birthday this week. Let's sing "Happy Birthday" for him. *(As the Cub Scouts sing,* DEN MOTHER *brings in birthday cake with nine lighted candles.)*

DEN MOTHER: Congratulations *(name)*. As you blow out the candles, we'll wish for you many happy days in Scouting.

DEN CHIEF: Will you come and stand by me *(name)?* You have worked hard and are now wearing the Wolf badge on your uniform. Now you are nine and ready to start earning your Bear badge. To help you, and with best wishes from all of us, here is your Bear book. We all know you will do your best and soon add the Bear badge to your uniform.

RECEIVING NEW MEMBER

Here is one occasion for which your boys may prefer to have a permanent ceremony. Perhaps it would be fitting for each boy to be welcomed into the den in the same way.

One way of doing this is to reserve one song for these welcoming occasions. Below are two sample welcoming songs.

WE'RE GLAD TO SEE YOU HERE
Tune: Farmer in the Dell
We're glad to see you here,
It gives us joy and cheer.
Sure, it's true, we say to you,
We're glad to see you here.

CUB SCOUT WELCOME SONG
Tune: Auld Lang Syne
We welcome you to our Cub den.
We're mighty glad you're here.
We'll start the air shaking
With a mighty cheer.

We'll sing you in; we'll sing you out,
For you we'll raise a shout.

Hail, hail, the gang's all here today,
You're welcome to our den!

Perhaps you as a Den Mother would also like to say a few words to the new boy about the den. Include a word about when the den was organized, the names of some of its former members, and some of the interesting things it has done.

You can end the welcome by having the Cub Scouts form a living circle (see page 127) with the new boy outside, then break the circle and invite the new boy to join.

Invite the new boy's mother to attend the first meeting. She'll enjoy the welcoming ceremony and have a chance to see what a den meeting is like.

Here is another ceremony to welcome a new Cub Scout, when he has earned his Bobcat pin. If your den has an artificial campfire (made with small logs, crushed red cellophane, and an electric light), use it in this ceremony.

DEN CHIEF (*to* DENNER): *(Name of new member)* is present and wants to join our den. Will you ask the den to be seated around our fire and bring *(name)* to the fire? (NEW CUB SCOUT *is escorted by the* DENNER.)

DENNER: Have you passed your Bobcat test with your parents?

NEW CUB SCOUT: I have.

DENNER: Tell us, what does the Cub Scout sign mean?

NEW CUB SCOUT: *(Tells his own meaning of the sign.)*

DENNER: Please give the Cub Scout Promise. (NEW CUB SCOUT *gives it.)* Give the Law of the Pack. *(The* NEW CUB SCOUT *does.)* You have learned well the ways of the Bobcat. We welcome you to Den *(no.)*. And now let's form the living circle with our new Cub Scout. *(Gives new member the handshake.)* Welcome, Bobcat.

TRANSFER TO THE WEBELOS DEN

When one of your Cub Scouts reaches his 10th birthday, he is usually transferred from your Cub Scout den into the Webelos den. The formal transfer ceremony is held at a pack meeting.

But the move from your den into the Webelos den is such an important step for the boy that it ought not to be passed over with-

out some simple ceremony in the den. Perhaps you might ask the denner to say a few words on behalf of the den about what fun they have had with the graduate. Since this will be his last meeting with your den, simple refreshments would add to the occasion. Also, you might invite the boy's mother. This will give you a chance to remind her that he will want her and his father on hand for the regular transfer ceremony at the next pack meeting.

To end the ceremony, the denner might read this poem:

We've played together and worked together,
Maybe had a fight or two.
We've taken trips and had some slips
And seen many projects through.
First a Bobcat, then a Wolf,
Next you earned your Bear degree.
And when you earn your Webelos,
A Boy Scout soon you'll be.
We hope you remember Den (no.) with delight.
We salute you! Good luck! Happy Scouting!

ADVANCEMENT CEREMONIES

The formal rituals marking advancement of a Cub Scout from Bobcat to Wolf and Wolf to Bear are held at pack meetings. However, there is no reason not to have a simple ceremony in the den to celebrate a member's advancement in rank.

The advancement ceremony in the den can be as simple as calling the boy up front, explaining to the den what he has achieved, then having the boys congratulate him with a cheer or a song. If your den has a den doodle, give him the privilege of tying to the den doodle whatever emblem you use to mark his advancement in rank. Also let him record his achievement on your Cub Scout Advancement Chart.

CLOSING CEREMONIES

Closing ceremonies are usually quiet and impressive. They may require more thought than other ceremonies. Occasionally, the Den Mother should include in the closing ceremony a simple thought. Don't preach a sermon, though. And don't overwork the Cub Scout Promise, Law of the Pack, or living circle.

Here are a few suggestions:

1. Cub Scouts and leaders form living circle. You or den chief says, "Do your best." Boys answer, "We'll do our best."
2. Turn the lights out, shine a flashlight on the flag, and sing "America."
3. Sing or hum a quiet song.
4. Boys form a circle around a lighted candle. Remind them of the cheer and feeling of friendship that even a small flame can spread. (No preaching beyond that.)
5. If your den has an artificial campfire, light it, and gather the boys around. Play a quiet recording.
6. Friendship circle. Each Cub Scout has a 3-foot section of rope joined with a square knot to that of the boy on his left. Boys hold rope with left hand and pull back to form a taut circle. You or the den chief says, "You are a part of a group of close friends, held together by the square knot—a symbol of being square. Let us give our Cub Scout Promise."
7. Circle song. Form a circle with arms around each other's shoulders and sing "Home on the Range" or "Cub Days."
8. A prayer. It should be suitable to all faiths unless all den members are of the same faith.

MISCELLANEOUS CEREMONIES

SPECIAL RECOGNITION.—There are times when a boy does something outside of Cub Scouting for which he may deserve recognition from his den. Perhaps a boy will win a prize at the school hobby show or in a community pushmobile derby. Perhaps he is a member of a championship baseball team or wins a prize for growing the best vegetable in a garden show.

A ceremony isn't necessary, but call the boy forward and tell the den what he has done during the week.

WELCOME-BACK CEREMONY.—When a boy has been ill or has been away from home for a period, welcome him back to his first den meeting with a brief welcome ceremony. It's an opportunity for a boy to feel important for a few minutes.

BOOK OF CEREMONIES.—Your guide to successful den ceremonies is *Staging Den and Pack Ceremonies*. Filled with all types of ceremonies for den and pack meetings, the book will give you valuable help in planning and staging your own den ceremonies, building props, and making costumes and equipment.

7. SONGS AND YELLS

It will be a rare den meeting when you won't plan to have at least one song or yell. A lively song or a rousing yell provides the perfect interlude after quiet, sit-down activities, giving the Cub Scouts a chance to work off stored-up energy before you turn to other projects. A quiet, impressive song sung to a tune like "Goodnight, Ladies," or a patriotic song may achieve a mood of unaccustomed thoughtfulness among your boys.

In this chapter, you will find just a sampling of songs and yells that suit different purposes. For good variety in your choice of songs, add a copy of the *Cub Scout Songbook* to your den library.

LEADING DEN SONGS

Either you, your assistant, or the den chief might be the regular song leader for your den, but don't rule out the potential leader among your Cub Scouts.

The song leader doesn't have to be an expert singer or conductor. One needs only the ability to carry a tune and some sense of keeping time. Your Cub Scouts won't mind (or perhaps even notice) an occasional sour note. So don't worry if you lack real musical ability; the main thing is to have fun. If your boys sense this, you'll get the response you want.

Here are a few hints for a song leader to keep in mind:

◆ Select songs to suit your purpose—rousing action songs to let off steam, quiet pensive songs, or inspiring patriotic songs.

◆ Lead off with a song everybody knows.

◆ Establish pitch by humming or singing softly, then louder so all can hear.

◆ Stop and start over if the den makes a bad start.

♦ Use hand motions to beat time and keep people together. Usually an up-and-down motion is enough.

♦ Teach songs at each den meeting, and you'll have a singing den at pack meetings. Decide on songs at the pack leaders' meeting; then all dens can practice the same ones.

Your Cub Scouts will know many songs like "Old MacDonald Had a Farm," "Row, Row, Row Your Boat," and "She'll Be Comin' 'Round the Mountain." These familiar songs are, of course, very good for den meetings. The songs listed below by categories may help you select suitable numbers. They are taken from the *Cub Scout Songbook* and are special Cub Scout songs boys will be glad to learn. Try them in your den.

GREETING SONGS

"We're Glad To See You Here," "Hello! Hello!" "How Do You Do?" "The More We Get Together," "We're Here for Fun."

HI! THERE, CUB!
Tune: Hail, Hail, the Gang's All Here

Hi! Hi! Hi! there, Cub!
We are glad to meet you,
We are glad to greet you.
Hi! Hi! Hi! there, Cub!
You are welcome to our den.

SONGS ABOUT CUB SCOUTING

"Akela's Pack," "Cub Days," "Cubs Whistle While They Work," "Cub Scout Booster Song," "Akela's Council," "Cubs Are Fair," "Cubs Are Square," "Cubbing in the Morning."

I'VE GOT THAT CUB SCOUT SPIRIT
Tune: Joy in My Heart

I've got that Cub Scout spi-rit,
Up in my head,
Up in my head,
Up in my head,
I've got that Cub Scout Spi-rit,

Up in my head,
Up in my head, to stay.
(Replace "head" with other words in last four verses.)
I've got that Cub Scout spi-rit,
Deep in my heart, etc.
(Continue as in first verse)
I've got that Cub Scout spi-rit
Down in my feet, etc.
I've got that Cub Scout spi-rit
All over me, etc.
I've got that Cub Scout spi-rit
Up in my head
Deep in my heart
Down in my feet
I've got that Cub Scout spi-rit
All over me
All over me, all ways.

FUN SONGS

"Be Kind to Your Web-Footed Friends," "There Were Three Jolly Fishermen," "John Jacob Jingleheimer Schmidt," "Ravioli," "Hail, Hail, the Gang's All Here," and "I Have a Dog."

THIS LITTLE CUBBING LIGHT

For the music, see *Cub Scout Songbook*

Action

Use action for lines 2, 3, and 4 as you sing each.

This little Cubbing light of mine, I'm goin' to let it shine,
This little Cubbing light of mine, I'm goin' to let it shine,
This little Cubbing light of mine, I'm goin' to let it shine,
Let it shine all the time, let it shine.

1. *Hold right forefinger up like a candle.*
2. All around the neighborhood.
2. *Move finger around in a square, and back to starting point.*
3. Hide it under a bushel—No!
3. *Place cupped left hand over the "light," then withdraw it quickly and shout, "NO!"*
4. Don't you "pfft" my little light out.
4. *In saying "pfft" you pretend to blow the light out.*

57

ROUNDS

"Come A-Hunting," "Down by the Station," "Little Tom Tinker," "Three Blind Mice," "Row, Row, Row Your Boat," "Sweetly Sings the Donkey," "Are You Sleeping?," and "Santa's Coming."

SHARP DEN SONG

Tune: Gillette Look Sharp March
To look sharp (clap) be a C-U-B
To feel sharp (clap) be a C-U-B
To be sharp (clap) be a Den _____ Cub
We're the best den in the U.S.A. (clap-clap)

ACTION SONGS

"Under the Chestnut Tree," "Little Peter Rabbit," "One Finger, One Thumb," "My Hat, It Has Three Corners," "Throw It Out the Window," "If You're Happy," "O Chester!," "The Damper Song," "The Grand Old Duke of York," "Head and Shoulders, Knees and Toes," and "Up the Ladder."

SHE'LL BE COMIN' 'ROUND THE MOUNTAIN

1. She'll be comin' 'round the mountain when she comes,
    Hoot, hoot!
Motion for pulling whistle cord

    She'll be comin' 'round the mountain when she comes,
    Hoot, hoot!
Same motion

    She'll be comin' 'round the mountain,
    She'll be comin' 'round the mountain,
    She'll be comin' 'round the mountain when she comes.
    Hoot, hoot!
Same motion

2. She'll be drivin' six white horses when she comes,
    Whoa, back!
Pulling back on reins

3. And we'll all go out to meet her when she comes,
    Hi, Babe!
Sweeping salute motion

4. And we'll kill the old red rooster when she comes,
    Hack, hack!
Chop wrist with side of hand

5. And we'll all have chicken 'n dumplings when she comes—
    Yum, yum!
Rub tummy

Directions

At the end of each verse, repeat in reverse order the motions of the preceding verses.

CLAP YOUR HANDS
Tune: Jingle Bells

Clap your hands! Clap your hands!
This is how it's done.
Clap your hands! Clap your hands!
To show you're having fun.
Stamp your feet! Stamp your feet!
Make a lot of noise.
Because we like so well to see-e-e-e-e
Such happy Cub Scout boys.

Music used by permission of Carl Fischer, Inc., New York.

ADVANCEMENT AND GRADUATION SONGS

WE'RE ON THE UPWARD TRAIL
We're on the upward trail,
We're on the upward trail,
Singing as we go. Scouting bound.
We're on the upward trail,
We're on the upward trail,
Singing, singing, ev'rybody singing.
Scouting bound.

NOTE—This song may be sung by two groups as a "round." The second group starts as the first group reaches the word "trail" in the second measure, skips the measure containing "ev'rybody singing," and joins the first group on the final "Scouting bound."

PATRIOTIC SONGS

"The Star-Spangled Banner," "America," "God Bless America," "America, the Beautiful," "Make America Proud of You," and "Columbia, the Gem of the Ocean."

FAREWELL SONGS

GOOD NIGHT, CUB SCOUTS

Tune: Good Night, Ladies

Good night, Cub Scouts.
Good night, Cub Scouts.
Good night, Cub Scouts,
We're going to leave you now.
Merrily, we Cub along, Cub along, Cub along.
Merrily, we Cub along,
Up the Cub Scout trail.
Sweet dreams, Cub Scouts.
Sweet dreams, Cub Scouts.
Sweet dreams, Cub Scouts,
We're going to leave you now.

SCOUTING WE GO

Scouting we go, Scouting we go,
Sunlit trails and lands where waters flow;
By the campfire's friendly flaming glow.
Scouting we go, Scouting we go.

THEME SONGS

"Train Song," "The Animal Fair," "Pinewood Derby Song," "We Are Den Number One" (*use at blue and gold banquet*), and "Smokey the Bear."

YELLS

In making up your den yell or yells, remember to make them simple and rhythmic. Yells should end on a word or phrase that the boys can fairly shout. Keep in mind that yells are primarily aimed at letting off steam at den and pack meetings. They may also help you develop and maintain den spirit.

Many football cheers that are familiar in your town can be adapted to den yells. Get your Cub Scouts into the act of creating yours; perhaps all of you together can compose a favorite yell or two. The more the boys help in composing the yell, the happier they will be to use it.

Here is an assortment of sample yells:

DEN ONE! DEN ONE!
Is there a better den?
None!
What den has most fun?
One!
Den One! Den One!

Two, four, six, eight,
Who do we appreciate?
Den One! Den One! Den One!
(Or two, three, four, etc.)

We'll do our best for the gold and blue!
We ARE the best! Den Two!

(Softly)
We're from Cub Scout Den 3,
And no one could be prouder;
And if you cannot hear us,
We'll shout a little louder!
(Repeat twice, louder each time)

Den Four! Den Four!
We are the Cubs in Den Four!
Once more!
Den Four!

One, two, three, four,
Which den do you cheer for?
Which den can you hear more?
Den Four! Den Four! Den Four!

F-I-V-E!
The den that's best for you and me!
Watch us go and you will see,
It's F-I-V-E!
Den Five!

Den Five, Den Five,
We're the den that is alive!
If you're good you will arrive,
In Den Five, Den Five!
Which den is really alive?
Which den has all the drive?
Den Five, Den Five, Den Five.

JOCKEY CHEER.—Cub Scouts stand facing denner, with knees slightly bent, caps on backwards. They clap hands on thighs and bounce up and down without moving feet, to imitate galloping horse. Denner waves hand and all shout "whoa" as they stop action. They then shout, "Cub Scouts! Cub Scouts! Cub Scouts!"

CHUGGING.—On signal, everyone calls out "Chug, chug, chug, chug," stressing the first "chug." This is repeated a number of times. Boys start slowly, then go faster and faster. They end with train whistle, "Hoot, hoot!"

8. GAMES

Boys like games—lots of them. They provide natural outlets for their competitive and physical urges. They give your den meeting an atmosphere of fun. That's why it's well to include at least two games at every meeting.

It's more natural for the den chief to lead games and it's more convenient, too. Just imagine yourself trying to demonstrate a wheelbarrow race or somersault race. If you had to do that you probably wouldn't feel much like participating in the rest of the den meeting.

You should be present during the games period, but coach your den chief so he can lead the games. If a game is not going as it should, try to correct the situation first by whispering a tip to the den chief. If things get out of hand, you will have to step in and take active leadership. But even in that case, keep your den chief in the picture so it looks as if he is helping, too.

TYPES OF GAMES

Your choice of games depends a great deal upon your meeting place. Even quiet games satisfy the urge for competition, but they do not provide an outlet for physical activity. Therefore, if your den meets in an apartment, it's wise to take your boys out to a park, driveway, play area, or school ground once in a while for games involving physical activity.

Remember, no matter where you meet, there are games that will fit your circumstances. Don't try a game unless it can be played easily at your meeting place.

In this chapter, you will find just a few games. For many more, add copies of *Games for Cub Scouts* and *Group Meeting Sparklers* to your den library. There are also excellent games in each issue of *Cub Scout Program Helps* and the *Den Chief's Denbook*. Another source is your local library.

The games in this chapter are divided into six types:

1. *Playways.*—These are special games which will help your Cub Scouts in mastering their achievements.

2. *Indoor games*

3. *Homemade games*

4. *Outdoor games*

5. *Dual contests*

6. *Games related to themes*

PLAYWAYS

Many of the achievement playways can be used in small quarters. Of course, you will not want to tell the Cub Scouts you are using the game to teach them something. Merely play it for the fun of playing. Remind them after the game that the things they did are related to one of the Cub Scout achievements or to Cub Scout skills and knowledge. An advantage of this type of game is that you can make up rules yourself so long as you give Cub Scouts the right sort of information about the achievements.

CUB SCOUT SALUTE RACE.—Conduct this race either indoors or outdoors. Select two teams, then conduct relay race in which each player salutes the den chief, the Den Mother, or the assistant Den Mother, one of whom is stationed in front of each team. Each boy salutes and touches off the next member. Some boys may salute more than once because the game continues until one team has executed 10 correct salutes. The leaders call aloud the numbers after each correct salute. They should be very strict.

SHOESTRING RELAY.—First, teach method of tying square bowknot—the correct shoestring tie—then choose sides and give each team time to practice. In relay fashion, one team runs to the Den Mother and the other to the den chief. If there is an odd number, use denner as judge. Arriving at designated spots, each player ties his shoestring and runs back to touch off the next player. Score one point for each correct tie and one extra point for the team that is first to tie a given number of correct knots. This relay is related to Wolf Achievement 8, Tying Things.

ANSWER HUNT.—Get your Cub Scouts to help you make flashcards. You need one for every letter of the alphabet except X, Y, and Z, which are seldom used in Cub Scouting. Make or get cards about 4 by 6 inches and print or paste one large letter on each card. On the back of each card, write your own questions. The first time you play the game you will need no more than one question for each card. The second time you play you can add more questions. Divide Cub Scouts into teams of two or three. The leader reads the question and then flashes the letter so Cub Scouts can see it. Each question must be answerable with one word or term which begins with the letter on the front of the card. The first group shouting out answer wins a point.

You can make up your own questions. Here are samples:

1. *On the back of card A write:* Tell the name of an important Cub leader beginning with this letter. *(Akela)*
2. *For letter B:* Something all Cub Scouts would like to become when they are old enough. *(Boy Scout)*
3. *For letter C:* Name of the pack leader. *(Cubmaster)*
4. *For letter E:* Name of Cub Scout elective. *(Electricity)*
5. *For letter F:* Something every Cub Scout should honor. *(Flag)*
6. *For letter G:* Something a Wolf Cub Scout makes and uses with his family. *(Games)*
7. *For letter T:* Common Cub Scout term for month's big idea. *(Theme)*
8. *Continue same . . .*

NOTE: Some of the games in this chapter are taken by permission from *Games and Game Leadership* by Charles F. Smith.

"OBSTICKLE" COURSE.—Have an obstacle course set up in advance for this meeting. Your den chief can help you plan a layout. The fun will be in adapting the obstacles to objects you can secure using the terrain of your outdoor area. Toward the end of the meeting hold the contests and races. Tell the Cub Scouts to practice these at home in preparation for another trail that will be made during the fourth den meeting of the month to determine who will represent the den in the pack contests.

Your obstacle course might go something like this: Do two front rolls; make a jump half turn and continue with two back rolls; pick up a ball and throw it 20 feet to a leader who throws it back; walk a 12-foot rail; do a "Tarzan rope swing" across an imaginary river; do three successive broad jumps; run to a leader who will hold the runner's ankles as he does three sit-ups; next, move to a chinning bar and do one pull-up; finally, run rapidly around the block and from a designated spot sprint the last 20 to 50 yards.

It would be good to have the den chief walk the entire den through the course, demonstrating and letting the Cub Scouts practice so they will understand the action required. "Obstickle" Course is related to Wolf Achievement 1, Feats of Skill.

INDOOR GAMES

HIDE THE CLOCK.—Start the game by blindfolding all of the Cub Scouts. Place an alarm clock with a fairly loud tick in the room. The first Cub Scout to find the clock and touch it by listening for the tick wins the game.

BLOWBALL.—Seat the Cub Scouts around a table small enough so they will be close together. Put a table tennis ball in the center of the table. On signal, the Cub Scouts, with their chins on the table and their hands behind them, try to blow the ball off the table between two of the other players.

BOTTLE THE CLOTHESPIN.—Place a milk bottle upright on the floor. Give each Cub Scout in turn 10 clothespins and have him stand over the bottle. Holding the pins at eye level, he tries to drop each one into the bottle. Keep score.

CHARADES.—Divide into two teams. Each team in turn chooses a word, song title, popular phrase, proverb, fairy tale, or comic-book character, and either singly or in groups acts out the chosen story or character. The other team tries to guess what is acted out. Most of the time people play this game in pantomime. If speaking seems necessary to make the meaning clear, talk.

NAIL-DRIVING CONTEST.—Provide each team with a piece of two by four wood, a hammer, and nails shorter than the thickness of the wood. Each Cub Scout drives two nails and then passes board and hammer to next player. The first team with all nails driven in straight wins.

POISON CIRCLE.—Draw a 2- to 3-foot circle on ground. Cub Scouts form a 4- to 5-foot circle around this inner circle and hold hands. The object of the game is to keep out of the inner circle while trying to force someone else in. Those touching the circle drop out. For an interesting variation, stand up two or three Indian clubs in place of the inner circle.

RAINY DAY BUTTON GAMES.—Make a miniature "golf course" by arranging nine cups on a covered table or short-napped

floor rug. Number the cups, Use buttons as in tiddledywinks to follow the course. Keep score for each hole as in golf.

Button football is played with goalposts (pencils in thread spools; string tied from post to post). One Cub Scout "kicks off." Other team has four snap jumps to get button across the goal line. If team scores, "ball" is "kicked" to other team. Score as in football.

A FISHING PARTY.—Try this game as an icebreaker gathering-time activity, or rainy day fill-in. Before the meeting starts, hide 50 or more cardboard fish in various parts of the meeting area. Have 10 each of salmon, shark, bass, haddock, and sardine. Each salmon "caught" counts 2 points; shark, 3 points; bass, 4 points; haddock, 5 points; and sardine, 10 points. As Cub Scouts arrive, invite them to fish in your indoor lakes for the next few minutes. When the fishing party is ended, participants count up their score. For fun, award the winner some inexpensive item such as a fishline and bobber or can of sardines.

PLINK, PLOP, CLUNK, BOING!—Here's a quiet game. It's a good indoor game. First, gather 12 or 15 different items such as an orange, a table-tennis ball, a peanut in its shell, a marble, a tennis ball, a beanbag, a piece of sandpaper, a piece of modeling clay, a penny, a quarter, a half-dollar, a domino.

Put all of the things on a table. Let everyone look at the objects for 1 minute. Then they must turn their backs to the table and be perfectly quiet. Now take one of the objects and, from a height of about 2 feet, let it fall to the table. Give each Cub Scout in turn a chance to name the object by its sound.

BALLOON BUSTER.—Each player is given a numbered balloon (paint on numbers after balloons are inflated). "It" is chosen and blindfolded. He stands in a circle made by the others, who hold hands. Then all the balloons are tossed into the center. While the players count to 50, "it" bursts as many balloons as he can. Players leave the circle as their balloons are burst. The owner of the last unbroken balloon wins the game.

OUCH.—This is a game of speed and is much funnier than it may sound. Cub Scouts are seated in a circle on the floor. The leader stands in the center. As the leader points toward each player, they call out numbers in succession. The first Cub Scout calls out 1; the second Cub Scout, 2; the third Cub Scout, 3; the fourth Cub Scout, 4. The fifth Cub Scout, instead of 5, says ouch. If he fails to do so and says 5, he is dropped from the game. The counting continues with ouch taking the place of every number which contains any multiple of 5 (10, 15, 20, etc.). The last Cub Scout remaining is the winner. Play the game fast, and skip from boy to boy to provoke confusion. To vary game, have Cub Scout who goofs take the place of the leader.

TARGET PRACTICE WITH GLIDERS.—Each Cub Scout makes a paper glider out of an 8½- by 11-inch sheet of paper. A target is drawn on wrapping paper and fastened across the top of a doorway. Openings are cut in the target and scored. Boys take turns sailing gliders. Best score in five chances wins.

FLYING SAUCERS.—See who can sail the most cardboard disks, one at a time, into a box 6 or 7 feet away.

SHOE RACE.—This is a good way to wind up a hilarious party. Each Cub Scout removes one shoe and places it on a pile at one end of the room. All line up at the opposite end. At signal, they hobble across the room, hunt for their shoes, put them on, and race back to the starting point. The first one to accomplish this gets a prize. For extra fun, hide two of the shoes.

HAND-SLAPPING HESSIAN.—Cub Scouts stand in a circle and hold with both hands a circle of strong cord or light clothesline. One stands in the center and is called "the Hessian." He endeavors to slap the hands of one of those holding the cord before they can be withdrawn. Whoever is not sufficiently alert and allows his hands to be slapped must take the place of the Hessian.

HOMEMADE GAMES

Homemade games are fun to make and play. They make fine father-and-son projects for family and den use. Sand wooden objects well and use bright-colored enamels.

BULLPEN PUZZLE.—Divide board into seven "pens" and number them in order, leaving the top square blank. Make six "bulls," numbering each. Place in pens in the order and play. Trick is to move bulls into their pens, at no time having more than one bull in each pen.

TABLE OR BOX HOCKEY.—Build box as illustrated and play as shown on page 73.

TIC-TAC-TREY.—Similar to ticktacktoe. Use 24 counters, 12 each of two different colors. Object is to get three in a row along a marked line while preventing your opponent from accomplishing this.

BALL TOSS.—Attach tin cans or cardboard containers to a board supported at an angle. Some may be grouped, others attached separately. Toss rubber balls into containers. If they bounce out, they do not score points.

QUOITS.—Make your own quoits from sections of a garden hose or rope. Make your goal by attaching a piece of broom handle to a base. For outdoor use, sharpen the end of a stake and drive it into the ground.

RING TOSS.—Screw curtain rod hooks into a board. Toss rubber jar rings.

OUTDOOR GAMES

TOUCH.—Divide the Cub Scouts into two teams and line them up across the center of the playing space facing each other, 6 or 8 feet apart. The object of the game is for the leader to name an object close at hand which all Cub Scouts must run and touch and then return to their original places.

The leader calls "touch" and pauses briefly before naming the object. "Touch a door!" The instant the object is named, all Cub Scouts break ranks, run and touch a door, and run back to their original places. The team wins whose members are back first.

KICK BASEBALL.—This game is much like regular baseball. The pitcher rolls a soccer ball or basketball underhand along the ground. The batter kicks the ball rather than using a bat. The runner may be put out by being hit with the ball as he runs the bases, or he may be put out just as in regular baseball.

The pitcher should roll the ball easily so the batter can successfully kick every pitch. Balls and strikes are not counted.

CIRCLE BALL KEEP AWAY.—Select "it" and provide him with a ball. Form the other Cub Scouts around him in a circle.

"It" starts the game by passing the ball to a Cub Scout on the circle who throws it to anyone else on the circle. The object of the game is for "it" either to catch or touch the ball while it is being passed about the circle. When "it" intercepts the ball, the Cub Scout who touched it last exchanges places with him.

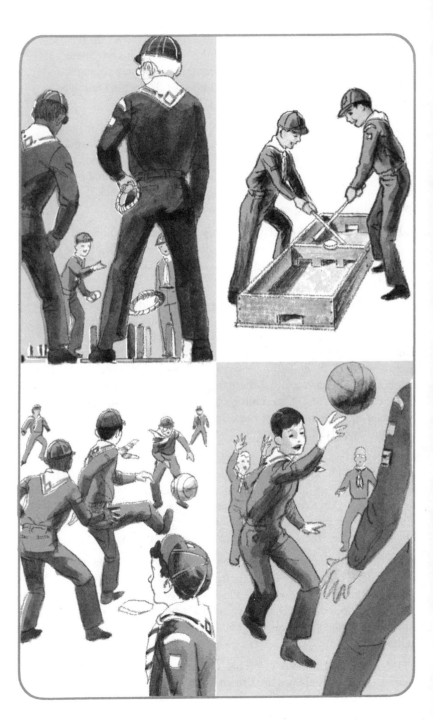

BALL CATCHING GO DOWN.—Line the Cub Scouts up side by side. The leader tosses or bounces the ball to each Cub Scout in turn. When his turn comes, a Cub Scout takes one step forward. If he catches the ball, he steps back into line. If he fumbles, he goes to the end of the line.

BALLOON KANGAROO RACE.—Cub Scouts stand in an even line, each with a 6-inch inflated balloon held between the knees. On signal they move along by hopping, for a distance of 40 feet, with both feet together and hands on hips. If the balloon breaks, the player is disqualified. If he loses it, he can pick it up, run back to the starting line, and start again.

CHASE ONE, CHASE ALL.—In this tag game, as soon as "it" tags someone, the two join in the pursuit of those untagged. Those tagged join the pursuers until last player is tagged. He becomes "it."

ANTE OVER.—Half of the den stands on one side of a garage, half on the other. While his team yells "ante, ante over," one of the boys throws the ball over the roof so it will run down the other side. If the ball doesn't make it, the team yells "back ball," and tries again. If the ball goes over, a player on the other team catches it; they dash around the garage after the first team. The Cub Scout who caught the ball tries to hit an opponent. An opponent who is hit must join the other side. The game continues until one side has all the players.

CHAIN TAG.—One Cub Scout is "it" and tries to tag one of the others. The Cub Scout tagged joins in the chase by holding hands with "it." They both now try to tag another player with their free hands. Each Cub Scout caught joins the tagging chain. Only the Cub Scouts on the ends may tag, and the tag doesn't count if the chain is broken. The last Cub Scout caught is "it" next.

TAILS.—The "tails" are neckerchiefs tucked under the belt, with at least two-thirds left hanging. The idea is to snatch the tail from the other fellow's belt. Play in a large circle or area with designated boundaries. Disqualify anyone who steps out. Winners are the ones who save their tails and the one who collects the most tails.

POM-POM-PULLAWAY.—This is one of our most popular games. Two parallel lines are drawn 50 to 150 feet apart at opposite ends of the yard. The players stand behind one of the lines.

The player who is "it" stands in the center. When "it" calls out, "Pom-pom-pullaway, if you don't come I'll pull you away," all players must run from one base across the clear space to the opposite base, while "it" attempts to tag one or more runners by slapping them three times on the back.

All who are tagged remain in the center and help catch the other players. When all are caught, the game starts over; the first one caught becoming "it" for the next game.

KILL THE RATTLER.—Two contestants, a hunter and a rattler, take their places in a circle surrounded by spectators. Both are blindfolded. The hunter is provided with a soft swatter—a stuffed stocking or rolled paper. The rattler has a covered can containing pebbles. The hunter starts the games by calling "rattlesnake"; whereupon, the rattler freezes on the spot, raises his head, and shakes his can of pebbles. The hunter hustles to the whereabouts of the snake and takes a crack at him. If he fails to hit him, the rattler crawls away and again the hunter calls, "rattlesnake," and then takes another try. This continues until he hits the snake. They then change places. There are two ways of scoring: The player wins who hits the other in the fewest tries; the one wins who hits his opponent the greater number of times in one or two minutes.

FRIENDLY ENEMIES.—This dual contest provides much more fun for the spectators than for the performers. It succeeds best when the combatants go after each other vigorously.

Two blindfolded antagonists are armed with swatters—a few sheets of newspaper rolled loosely or a stuffed stocking. They stand any way they please, grasping extended left hands. To start the contest, one of them asks the other, "Where are you, friend?" His opponent either ducks down or sways backward or sideward, and while in that position answers, "I'm here." The other listens and notes the apparent spot from which the voice comes and takes a swat at his "friendly enemy." If he strikes him above the shoulders, he receives one point. Opponents alternate in calling and striking. They continue until one scores two or three points.

BALLOON OR BAG BURSTING.—There are several variations of the old-time favorite. In the simplest type just give each boy a balloon or bag and have the boys blow them up at the word "go." The first one to blow it up so it bursts wins.

An even more interesting balloon-bursting contest is one in which balloons are blown up until they are equal in size, then tied to the end of a 2-foot string. The other end of the string is tied to the boy's ankle. At the word "go," each boy tries to break the other boy's balloon by stepping on it. Leaders should be alert to the need for a short rest period if boys appear tired.

DUAL CONTESTS

HAND PUSH.—Two Cub Scouts face each other with toes touching and palms together at shoulder height. Each tries to push the other's hands until he is forced one step back.

BROOMSTICK TWIST.—The two Cub Scouts should be about equal in height and weight. They grasp a broomstick held horizontally with both hands. Each tries to touch the end of the broomstick to the floor on his right.

COCKFIGHT.—Two Cub Scouts hold their left ankles with left hands, and keep their right arms close to their sides. On signal they try to upset each other by charging or shouldering. The player who falls or lets go of his ankle is the loser. A free-for-all cockfight can be held with all the boys in the den. The last player still standing and holding his ankle is the winner.

PULL OVER.—Boy braces feet, grasps right hand of his opponent with his own right hand, and tries to pull him over a center-line on the ground. Vary by changing hands.

SACK FIGHT.—Each boy stands in a burlap or similar type of bag. He must use both hands to keep the bag stretched to its full length. He tries to upset others by thrusting and pushing with shoulders and hips. This can be a dual contest or a mass battle where boys are eliminated as they lose their balance and fall.

GAMES RELATED TO MONTHLY THEMES

Often games will fit into the theme for the month. This serves to keep the boys interested in the theme. You generally find such games suggested in *Cub Scout Program Helps*. Here are a few examples of this type of game. In each case we mention the theme to which the game is related.

FOR ANIMALS AND PETS THEME—BEAST, BIRD, FISH. —Divide the Cub Scouts into teams A and B. Seat teams opposite

each other in two parallel lines. An A member starts the game by throwing an object such as a knotted handkerchief, softball, or beanbag to any B member, calling as he throws, one of the words, "beast" or "bird" or "fish." The instant after calling, he starts to count 10. Before he reaches 10, the B player must name a beast or bird or fish, depending upon what the A player called. If the B player fails to do so before the thrower counts 10, one point is scored for team A. Similarly, a point is scored if an object already named is mentioned a second time.

The teams throw alternately, the winner being the team ahead at the end of a time limit. It adds to the fun to permit a player who cannot think of a name quickly to throw the handkerchief to a teammate at least two players distant and call "help!"

FOR LIFE IN THE PHILIPPINES THEME— BUNONG BRASO.—This game is a sport common among Filipino boys and a favorite of our own. Two Cub Scouts sit across from each other at a table. They grasp right hands and put their right forearms against each other. The object, of course, is to down your opponent's arm without lifting your elbow from the table or using anything but the strength of your one arm.

FOR KNIGHTS OF YORE THEME—BATTLE ROYAL.— This is a mass battle with each contestant holding a broomstick horse in one hand and swinging a weapon (such as stuffed sock) in the other. Each Cub Scout wears a paper hat and leaves the contest when he loses his hat.

FOR IN OLD MEXICO THEME—IN SHE GOES.—Here is a homemade scoop—the game will remind you of Mexican *jai alai*. It is sure to become a favorite activity for the informal part of any meeting. The game is played with a whiffle ball and scoops made from half-gallon plastic bleach bottles. Den is divided into teams of three or four Cub Scouts. The ball cannot be touched by the hand. It is caught and thrown by the scoop. Boys can use this equipment to play variations of keep away, catch, or hockey.

For hockey you will need a large area. Goals are set up. To start, one team throws as far into opponent's area as possible. Team members pass the whiffle ball between them and try to throw it into their opponent's goal. The opponents try to intercept and then attempt to score themselves.

Team scored on puts whiffle ball in play as in basketball. Make up your own variations and rules. It's all fun.

FOR TRANSPORTATION THEME — TRAIN RELAY.— Dens line up for relay. First Cub Scout runs to finish line, comes back, and touches next Cub Scout, who hitches on. Then both go to the line and return. Third boy hitches on, etc. The last Cub Scout is the caboose. He must hitch on backwards.

FOR TRAILBLAZERS THEME—ANIMAL HUNT.—Hide small objects such as animal cutouts or wrapped pieces of candy around the room. Form two teams—the "ducks" and the "sheep" —each with a leader. On signal individual players begin hunting for the hidden objects. But only the leader may do the retrieving. When a duck discovers an object, he "quacks" loudly to attract the attention of his leader. Sheep "baa" for their leader. If the group is large, form additional teams of "crows" or "donkeys." The team that recovers the most objects in 5 minutes wins.

FOR HOLIDAY THEME—I SPY SANTA.—Before the group arrives, hide a small figure or picture of Santa Claus in the room. Announce that Santa is somewhere in the vicinity and everyone is to look for him. When a Cub Scout locates Santa, he should not give away the location but whisper it to the leader, be seated, and watch the others look. (Other figures may be used. For example, Daniel Boone could be the subject for January; George Washington for February.)

FOR AMATEUR HOUR THEME—A TALENT SHOW.— "Watch me" is a favorite plea of boys. A talent show provides an opportunity for adults to watch from an easy chair while the Cub Scouts perform. The talent show gives the boy acrobat, magician, singer, or musician a chance to show off. It would be fun if moms and dads put on an act, just to join in. Lip singing, for example, is a good trick. (Put on a vocal record, mouth the words, and make appropriate gestures.)

9. HANDICRAFT

"How do you get Cub Scouts to do their work? I give them something to do before the next den meeting; then, when the meeting comes, they have not completed their assignments."

That's what one Den Mother said. She seemed to be quite disturbed and surprised over the fact that the Cub Scouts did not complete their assignments. This is not surprising. Frankly, it sounds a little too much like work.

Another Den Mother confided that she had "failed miserably" in getting her Cub Scouts interested in handicraft.

"For example," she said, "I cut out of a magazine a lively diagram for a dog doorstop. It was made in the form of a bulldog and was to be painted white with black spots. My husband made a sample and I tried to interest my boys in making one like it.

"Their attitude was most disappointing. One boy said he had a cocker spaniel and that if he was going to make a doorstop, it was going to be a cocker spaniel. Another boy said that he had a cat, and that he would like to make a cat doorstop. Two boys didn't even want to make a doorstop!"

That Den Mother, too, should not have been surprised at the reaction of her boys. Boys of Cub Scout age, especially the younger ones, are individualists. They have their own ideas and they like to have their say in deciding what they are going to do.

THE REASONS FOR CRAFTS

Handicrafts are not used in Cub Scouting merely to provide "busy work" for the boys to keep them out of the Den Mother's hair. There are several excellent reasons for craftwork, the most important being that most Cub Scouts enjoy making things.

Craftwork also gives the boys a chance to use and thus develop their fertile imaginations and to improve their skills in handling tools. It is important to encourage the natural creative urge in a

boy. Unless you do, the urge may disappear and be replaced by a lack of confidence. Your job as a Den Mother is to stimulate each Cub Scout's interest and curiosity and encourage and help him to try more difficult projects.

Cub Scouts are boys—red-blooded American boys who like to run and jump, yell and pound, or walk the plank just as did the pirates' captives of years ago. Cub Scouts need boy crafts that help them grow in skills and desirable attitudes. They need hammering, sawing, and painting—not cutting and pasting.

You, your assistant Den Mother, and your den chief share the work of teaching the Cub Scouts how to use tools and in helping them with crafts.

Chances are you will be more skilled than the den chief in crafts involving cloth, paper, and paints, but he should be a big help in teaching the Cub Scouts how to use tools and in helping them with crafts.

Cub Scout craftwork is done for either:

♦ A project connected with the pack's monthly theme, or
♦ A project required to pass an achievement or elective, or
♦ Just for fun.

CRAFTS AND THE THEME

In your den, most of the crafts probably will concern the monthly theme, because as a general rule the boy works on achievements and electives in his own home with the help of his parents. (Selection of monthly themes is explained in chapter 13, "Your Program—Who Plans It.")

The monthly theme is designed to suggest wide areas of activity for the dens, including craftwork. This gives you and your boys an opportunity to use your imaginations about what to make.

If the theme is good, it will open up a great variety of activities. Each boy may select something to make which has special appeal for him. For example, instead of trying to get every Cub Scout in the den to make a kite during Things That Fly month, it would be far more effective to let each make his own choice. This stimulates each to use his own imagination. Things that fly might include not only kites, but also paper gliders, flying model planes, nonflying plane models, and boomerangs.

In Cub Scouting we don't start out by saying, "What shall we make?" First we work out the theme. Then, in the process of being something, or acting the part of somebody, we make something. What we make will depend on what we are trying to be. If it's King Arthur, we'll make things that relate to knights. If it's Indian month, we'll make such things as tepees, shields, tomahawks, and headdresses, each boy choosing the things which interest him.

Does that mean that the whole den should never make the same things? No, of course not. There may be times when every boy will make the same thing. However, the whole craft program should not be built around that idea. In other words, handicraft most often comes out of a theme rather than being treated as craft for the sake of craftwork.

What if one of your Cub Scouts wants to make something not connected with the theme at all? Let him. Johnny may want to make a leather belt during Things That Fly month, and he won't understand why he can't, just because you say it's the wrong month for belts. Chances are when he sees the fun the others are having making things that fly, he'll want to join in, too. And he still can go ahead with his leather belt.

A TYPICAL THEME AND ITS CRAFT POSSIBILITIES.— Let's imagine that the theme in your pack for the current month is When Dad Was a Boy, built around the idea of doing the things that dad once enjoyed doing. There are plenty of craft opportunities in the theme without making it necessary for the Den Mother to develop additional projects. At the first den meeting the theme is explained to the boys. They are encouragd to go home and talk to their dads about the theme and get their dads to teach them their favorite boyhood puzzle or feat of magic. Each dad helps his son to make the magic trick or puzzle. The boys demonstrate these at the next meeting.

At the second den meeting each boy is encouraged to get his dad to help him make something that dad himself enjoyed making as a boy. One dad shows his son how to make the equipment for wheel-racing, a pastime most present-day boys have never experienced. Other dads and sons make tetherball games, pushmobiles, and roller-skate scooters.

In the third den meeting each boy is encouraged to get his dad to show him his most interesting boyhood hobby or pastime. Many of these hobbies involve crafts. In some cases they are collections, which have to be mounted. In one case, a dad may have enjoyed making waterwheels as a boy, so he and his son reproduce an old-fashioned mill and waterwheel.

There are many other projects too numerous to mention. However, you see that the theme is the important thing. If the theme is good, it will provide many opportunities for interesting crafts, but they will be crafts with a purpose.

DADS AND HANDICRAFT

Try to start some of your craft projects in your den meetings, but have the boys complete them at home with the help of their dads. Not only does this relieve you of some of the responsibility for crafts, but it also draws the dad into the program. As in everything else, the first time is the most difficult for dad. After he has worked with his boy on several items, he will begin to enjoy it and to appreciate the closer relationship with his son.

Sometimes projects can be handled completely in the home. One Den Mother in the month of September was eager to do something to improve her den meeting place. She talked it over with her Cub Scouts. They decided it would be nice if each boy worked with his dad in making a chair for use in the den meetings. So the Den Mother had each boy write a note to his dad suggesting that they work together on this project using an orange crate, nail keg, or anything else available at home. There was no attempt on the part of the Den Mother to have all the chairs alike.

Another pack was having a pack circus. Two of the dens chose to make animals. One Den Mother tried to do the whole job. She collected the material, drew the plans, and supervised the construction—all in den meetings. She was quite worn out after the circus and was heard to say, "Well, Cub Scouting is a wonderful thing, but the parents certainly do not take much interest in what their boys are doing."

In the other den that made animals, the Den Mother went at it in a different way. She got each boy with his dad to choose an animal they would make together. Then she asked the den dad to phone the other dads and ask them to help their boys in making the animals. As a result the six boys had wonderful circus animals, far better in quality than those produced by the other den.

And by the way, that circus project is another good example of something we talked about a little earlier in this chapter—the theme is the thing. You see, it would be unnecessary to make unrelated projects when the circus itself opens up so many handicraft possibilities. It isn't a matter of "let's do some handicrafts," but "let's have a circus."

DADS WITH SPECIAL ABILITIES.—In practically every den you will find a few dads who have special hobbies or abilities which will be particularly helpful to the den. While they can't attend regular den meetings, they can cooperate with you on special projects.

One pack recently had a pinewood derby, and each boy was to make a car. A dad in one den was quite familiar with this type of project, so he invited all of the other dads of the den over to his home one evening and showed them how to make a pinewood racer with their sons.

While you can't do this every month, it's a good method to keep in mind for some special occasion where dads will need help and encouragement.

The one person who can help you more than anyone else with special projects is your den dad. He can be of special help to you in getting materials for crafts. Usually the materials are paid for by the pack treasury, but someone must do the buying and handle the details. Let the den dad help with this.

COMPETITION IN CRAFTS

Normally it is very unwise to conduct handicraft competitions. There is little sound basis for judging one boy against another. Boys need recognition and they need successful experience. They can get both of these in Cub Scout handicrafts without competition.

The difficulty in handicraft competition is that the judges normally know little about the background of the boys whose work they are judging. One boy's project may look poor and another's look wonderful. It's possible, however, that the boy who made the poor project has accomplished a great deal. It may be the first thing he has actually made with his own hands. In that case, the main objective should be to encourage the boy and his parents. It's bad to do that on a competitive basis, because unfortunately you have to recognize the better project, not the better effort.

HOW MUCH CAN YOU EXPECT?

The way in which a boy performs in a given project is determined largely by his interest in the project. If it is something he selected of his own free will, you naturally can expect him to carry through with more enthusiasm. As often as possible, then, let boys choose their own projects.

Guard against measuring the boy's craft efforts with an adult measuring stick. In Cub Scouting we must revise our adult standard of measurement so it fits the boy. We must expect neither too little nor too much, because either is undesirable. This imposes no easy task upon a dad, but it will help if he spends a bit of time looking back on his own boyhood.

Our real task is to keep the boy always reaching higher and at the same time to give him a feeling of success and satisfaction in what he is doing at a given moment. The parent or den leader who expects too much may build up frustration within the boy.

The first approach, then, should be to compliment the boy for what he has done. Then, perhaps, through conversation the Den Mother or dad can suggest ways to improve the project. But dad must not stop there. His suggestion for improvement will be far more effective if he rolls up his sleeves and spends a few minutes helping the boy toward such improvements—but not doing it all for him!

The average 8-year-old boy seems to minimize his own efforts. He may often be heard to say, "That's not much good, is it, dad?" Of course, when the boy says such a thing he is sometimes hoping to give dad an opportunity to assure him that what he has done is worthwhile. Simple recognition and the experience of tasting success are vital to a boy's development.

TOOLS AND MATERIALS

Your den does a great many craft projects with just a few simple tools. Each Cub Scout should have some of his own, marked with his name and initials, which can be stored in individual boxes or a den tool chest. Include for each boy:

◆ Pencils and crayons
◆ Watercolors and brushes
◆ Light hammer
◆ Blunt-nose scissors
◆ Ruler (12-inch)
◆ Small knife

You should have as many of the following tools and supplies as possible for the entire den to use. Parents may donate or loan most of them, either permanently or as they are needed. Others

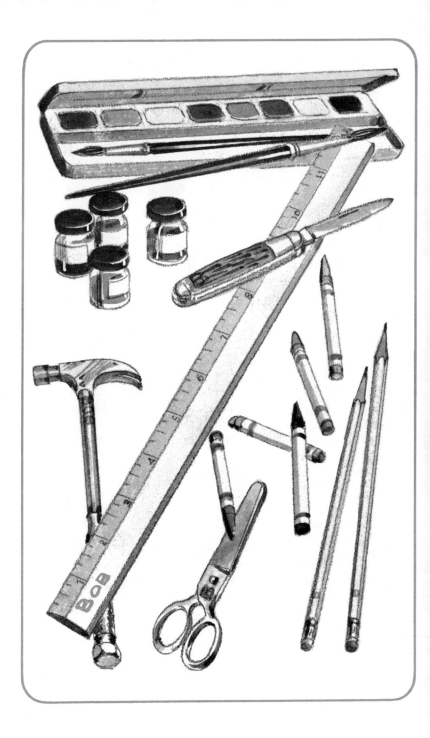

may be bought for the den from pack funds. You and the den chief are, of course, responsible for keeping track of them.

- Assorted nails, beads, pins, screws, tacks
- Paper paste or rubber cement and wood glue
- Wood of various shapes and sizes. (White pine is easy to whittle.)
- Paper and cardboard boxes of various sizes and colors
- Balls of cord, string, and small rope
- Wire. (Ask telephone repairmen for scraps of small covered wire.)
- One or two hammers
- Pliers with wire cutters
- Screwdrivers
- Combination 26" saw and one or two coping saws
- Hand drill
- Palm or block plane
- One or two wood rasps and files
- Sandpaper

Keep a scrapbox handy for the den's collection of old spools, bottle tops, clock works, bits of hardware, doorknobs, dowels, aluminum foil, scraps of rubber inner tubes, plywood, leather, wheels, metal, toy parts, and other things that might be used in crafts. Watch for construction and remodeling projects. A little visit with the person in charge can result in a real windfall.

If you have space in your den meeting place, the boys might make their first craft project—a workbench.

IDEAS AND PLANS

Most of the ideas for handicrafts in your den will come from the boys as they think about the month's theme. When they have an idea, you may help them get started by finding plans for the items they want to make in one of the following sources:

- *Wolf Cub Scout Book*
- *Bear Cub Scout Book*
- *Cub Scout Fun Book*
- *Cub Scout Activities*
- *Crafts for Cub Scouts*
  Ask your librarian for books on crafts.

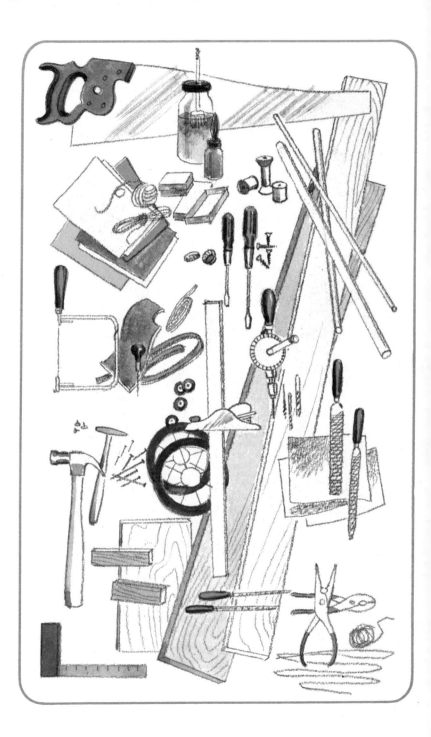

10. STUNTS AND SKITS

Very often—perhaps each month—your den will be preparing a stunt or skit to present at the monthly pack meeting of Cub Scouts and parents.

The words "stunt" and "skit," as they are used in Cub Scouting, are almost synonymous. A stunt might be a pantomime or simple trick, while a skit is a sketch or short play; the point of both is fun for the boys and the audience.

Usually, your skit will be based on the pack's monthly theme. Probably each den in your pack will be working on something similar for the pack meeting. If all dens have prepared well, the boys and parents are in for a most amusing pack meeting.

If the month's theme has captured the imagination of your den, you will get lots of help from the Cub Scouts themselves in planning your skit. But almost certainly you will have to direct the planning, conduct the rehearsals, and approve the final preparations. Your den chief ought to be a big help, both in preparing and in staging your skit on pack meeting night. He can help secure props (keep them as simple as possible) and serve as stage manager. Whenever possible, call on your assistant Den Mother, den dad, and other parents to help.

If you have had no training in dramatics, all this may scare you off. Don't let it; it's not that serious. The idea is fun for your boys and the parents.

PREPARING A SKIT

There are four things to keep in mind when your den is preparing a skit:

1. Keep it short (from 3 to 5 minutes).
2. Avoid having a lot of dialogue.
3. Use simple props.
4. Give each boy in the den something to do.

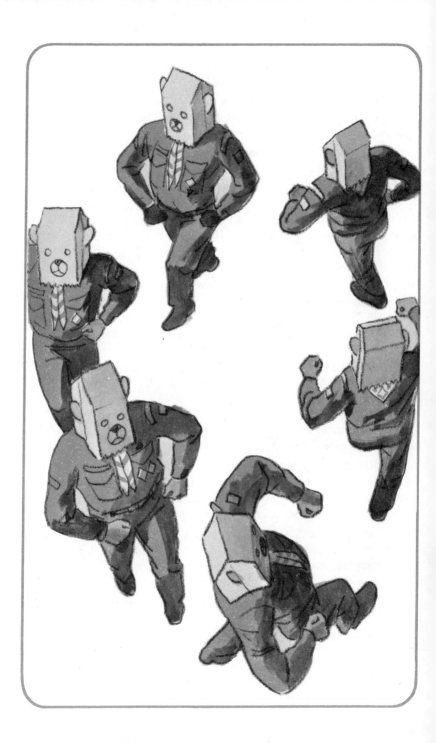

The first few pages of the *Skits and Puppets* booklet contains some excellent suggestions on developing skits. Throughout the rest of that booklet, leaders will find many ready-to-use skits. Others may be found in your local library.

Avoid skits that ridicule persons or groups. They are in bad taste and aren't worth the time it takes in preparation.

Martin Stevens of Middlebury, Ind., one of America's foremost puppeteers, says:

"A play is merely the exposition of the experience of a character who wants something very much and tries to get it. Something or someone hinders him, and for a time makes it seem that he will never get his desire. But then a decision he makes and an action he takes overcomes the hindrance, and he gets what he wanted. It's that simple! Classically stated, 'Boy meets girl, boy loses girl, boy gets girl.' Just look at any play with which you're familiar and see how it goes: *Cinderella, Red Riding Hood, Snow White.* Name your own. Now take a soap commercial: Lady has lovely hands, lady uses strong detergent and loses lovely hands, lady uses OUR detergent and again has lovely hands! Take a welfare campaign: Human has right to health and happiness, human loses health and happiness, but through YOUR contribution, human gets health and happiness. See how it works? Punch has life, liberty, and the pursuit of happiness; hangman threatens to remove all three; Punch hangs the hangman and regains life, liberty, and the pursuit of happiness.

The first thing you need for a skit is an idea. Hopefully, your Cub Scouts will have some suggestions for a skit as you talk over the month's theme. You may have to prod their imaginations with a few tentative suggestions; but once started, the ideas will come.

For example: Let's say the theme is Cowboys. Now, what springs to mind when we think of cowboys? Cattle, the open range, campfires, rodeos. Ah, rodeos! Your Cub Scouts may never have seen a rodeo, but they probably know it includes riding and roping contests for cowboys. Plenty of drama in a rodeo.

Many themes will suggest skits based on history. For a Mountains of America theme, for example, skits could be based on the adventures of such mountain men and explorers as Kit Carson or Daniel Boone. Often, with a theme of this sort, local history can be brought into focus for the Cub Scouts. In such cases, you may have to provide the stimulus for the skit unless the character on which it will be based is very well known, but the fact that it is about the history of their own region will spur the Cub Scouts to greater effort to stage a good skit.

HELPING YOUR DEN DEVELOP A SKIT

Let's say the theme is South America. At your first den meeting use a blackboard or a large piece of cardboard on which you will develop ideas for the skit.

Establish the place: South America

Set the time: Any date in history

Below are four steps to present to the boys to develop your skit. Place these in a column and leave space for suggestions.

1. Boy wants something—   (Boys Suggest)
Friendship
A gold mine
A game trophy
Find a lost civilization or some-place else.

2. Boy starts to get it—

By canoe
Plane
Horseback
On foot
Right at home
By using his brain
Some other way.

3. Obstacles stop boy—

Crocodile
Native headhunters
Secret enemy
A false friend
Any other problems.

4. Boy achieves goal—

Through an act of kindness
Bravery
Wisdom
Magic
Unexpected help
Some other way.

MAKE IT FUN

What makes a good den skit for a pack meeting? One that is fun for both actors and audience—simple, short, with little dialogue to memorize, props and costumes that are simple, and enough roles so that each boy in the den has one. Rhyming of words may make it somewhat easier for boys to memorize parts, but rhyming is, of course, not at all necessary.

You probably will want to write at least an outline for your den skit. If you do, bear in mind that your dialogue must be broad and simple enough for Cub Scouts to understand and speak, and that the point or joke of the skit ought to be broad and simple, too. Make sure that each of your Cub Scout actors knows where he should be at each point in the skit and what he should be doing.

If the boys in your den enjoy making and working with puppets, you could give a skit using puppets in place of Cub Scouts at a pack meeting. An occasional puppet show at den meetings would be fun. You will find instructions for making and working with puppets in *Skits and Puppets*.

PREPARING A STUNT

The same principles apply to den stunts as to skits. In a stunt you are unlikely to have much dialogue, but the other things to remember are the same:

♦ Keep it short.

♦ Use simple props.

♦ Give each boy something to do.

If the month's theme was Indians, your den might have made a tepee and some tomahawks, tom-toms, headdresses, and other Indian paraphernalia. For your pack entertainment, then, it would be easy to prepare an Indian dance as your stunt, using all the props the den had made during the month. (You'll find an Indian dance illustrated in Elective 10 in the *Wolf Cub Scout Book*.)

For a circus theme, your den could have an educated horse (Cub Scout with a paper-bag horse's head); a fat lady, a strong man, or a tightrope walker (who walks a rope stretched on the floor); and a giant (a Cub Scout on stilts).

PANTOMIMES.—Cub Scouts are at the age when most boys enjoy playing make-believe. Watch them when they are at unsupervised play outdoors. Chances are you'll hear one say, "Let's

play like we're . . ." and the whole gang is instantly transformed into horses or spacemen or spies. Notice that it is not so important what they *say*. It is what they do.

They are pantomiming. Pantomimes make good den stunts because they are easy to prepare and perform. Your younger Cub Scouts, especially, may have trouble memorizing dialogue. If they do, plan pantomimes for your stunts.

You can add to the fun of pantomimes if you put them on with no introduction and let the audience guess what they saw.

Make costumes for pantomimes, if they are needed, out of readily available materials—blankets, bed sheets, scarves, wrapping paper, newspaper, or cardboard cartons. The simpler the better. Rope, cloth, or colored paper make good wigs, masks, or hats. Keep in mind, however, that costumes are a minor part of pantomime. Gestures and facial expressions are much more important.

Historical episodes make excellent subjects. Try Custer's Last Stand, the Battle of Bull Run, or the Battle of Tippecanoe.

GROWING MACHINE.—Find a cardboard carton large enough to hold a boy. Dress him in baby clothes. Equip the box with imitation cranks, levers, and dials. The "inventor" explains that he will now demonstrate his growing machine. He drops in a baseball; the hidden boy throws out a basketball. He drops in some string; out pops rope, and so forth. Finally, he drops in a baby doll. Out pops the hidden boy himself, who runs to the inventor shouting, "daddy, daddy!"

HAIRCUT MACHINE.—A boy wearing a large wig enters the "barbershop" and asks for a haircut. The barber asks him to stick his head in the haircut machine (a large box). The boy puts his head in the box, and there is much yelling, accompanied by sounds of machinery. The boy switches his wig for a bathing cap. He then removes his head from the machine and runs wildly offstage.

THE STORY AND DANCE OF BALOO.—Baloo the bear was the animal in *The Jungle Book* by Kipling. He taught the law of the jungle to Mowgli. He was the wise, good-natured, burly old fellow, very much like a big policeman.

For this dance, form a circle and, when the order "Baloo" is given, every Cub Scout follows the leader, marching very slowly and stiffly, with his stomach forward and his elbows stuck out, chin in the air, looking left and right in a stern way.

As the leader walks along, he recites the Law of the Pack in a loud voice so that everyone shall know it. The Cub Scouts repeat each line of the Law as he gives it. "The Cub Scout follows Akela —the Cub Scout helps the pack go—the pack helps the Cub Scout grow—the Cub Scout gives goodwill."

When Akela gives the signal, all stand at attention. Akela says "Do your best." Cubs yell back, "We'll do our best," and go to their places.

A musical background such as "The Teddy Bear Picnic" or the "Policeman's Chorus" from the "Pirates of Penzance" will help create the right atmosphere.

IDEAS AND PLANS

As was noted in the beginning of this chapter, your Cub Scouts should be called upon for ideas for stunts and skits and for the way they want to work them out. Undoubtedly, they will need your help. Here are good sources of ideas and suggestions for skits, stunts, pantomimes, and puppets:

♦ *Skits and Puppets*
♦ *Den Chief's Denbook*
♦ *Cub Scout Program Helps*

11. TRICKS AND PUZZLES

Magic and mystery.

Those are two surefire words to capture a Cub Scout's fancy. Almost everyone enjoys a trick or puzzle, and no one more than an 8- or 9-year-old boy.

Either you or the den chief will want to have a new trick or puzzle to show your Cub Scouts at almost every den meeting. Or, perhaps each of your Cub Scouts will learn a new trick with his dad before a meeting to show to the den. First he tries to fool his den mates, then he teaches them the trick, and they in turn go home and try to fool their families with it.

No matter who shows them, you'll find tricks and puzzles very popular additions to your den meeting plans. Obviously, they must be simple enough so that young boys can do them themselves. Puzzles ought to be the type which boys can make.

Here is an assortment of good tricks and puzzles for Cub Scouts. They're all simple, fun to learn, and mystifying.

THE VANISHING SUGAR LUMP.—Place a cup over a lump of sugar and say that you will make the sugar vanish without touching the cup. Move a hand over the cup and say, "That's all." Wait until a Cub Scout lifts the cup to see whether the sugar has vanished. Then take the lump and eat it.

Say, "It's gone, and I didn't touch the cup."

THE DISAPPEARING COIN.—For this trick, you need a helper—perhaps the den chief or denner.

Hold up a coin between your left thumb and first finger and then cover it with a handkerchief. With the right thumb and first finger, take the coin and handkerchief away from the left hand. Your right hand will now be outside the handkerchief and holding the coin through it. Ask a Cub Scout to put his hand under the handkerchief and touch the coin as shown.

Ask another Cub Scout or two to touch the coin to make sure it's still there. Have your helper—the den chief or denner—be the LAST to reach under the handkerchief. He takes it out with his fingers and looks as mystified as the rest when, after saying a few magic words, you throw the handkerchief into the air and the coin has disappeared.

THE MAGNETIZED PENCIL.—Use a pencil or ruler that is long enough to be seen from both ends when it is in your hand. Let the Cub Scouts see you close the fingers of one hand on the pencil and then turn the back of this hand to them. With the other hand, take hold at the wrist. Say that you have to hold the hand with the pencil very steady. Slowly, open and spread your fingers. The pencil will be seen as though it were sticking to your hand. The secret. Before you open your hand, slide the first finger of the hand holding the wrist onto the pencil.

For added mystery, rub the pencil against your sleeve to "magnetize" it before starting the trick.

THE DISAPPEARING KNOT.—Hold both ends of a 3-foot-long rope in your left hand. Put your right hand under and through the bend. Bring your right hand holding the two rope parts back through the bend to make the two loops as shown.

Put the ends in your left hand through both loops. Let go with the left and take hold of one end.

Take the other end in your right hand and pull ends apart. When small knot forms, blow on it and pull the rope straight.

MATCH MATH.—Ask your Cub Scouts how much 5 added to 6 makes. They will tell you 11 (at least we hope they will). Tell them you will add 5 matches to 6 and make 9. The drawing shows how it's done. (Toothpicks, twigs, or pencils can be used.)

HYPNOSIS LIFT.—You will need four people as lifters, one chair, and one volunteer. With volunteer sitting on a chair, the four lifters stack right hands and then left hands on head of volunteer. They then exert a slight downward pressure, quickly remove hands, and lace fingers together with forefingers extended. Two lifters place extended fingers under volunteer's armpits. Two place fingers under his knees. On count of three, they raise him.

RISING STARS.—Two Cub Scouts, arms interlocked, sit back to back on the floor and try to get on their feet. Several teams compete. Team requiring least time wins.

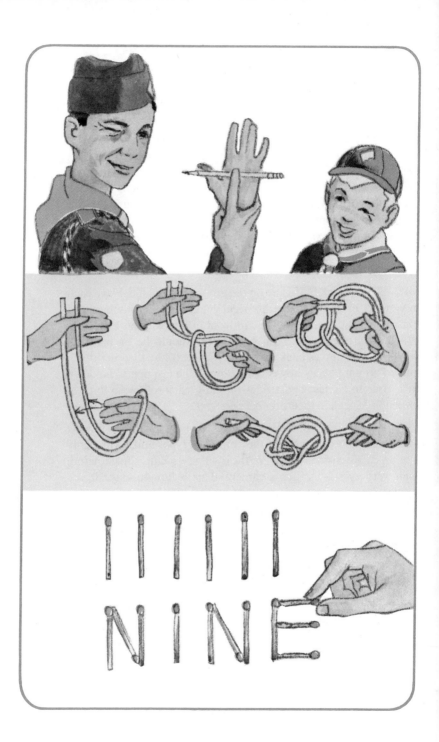

TIGHTROPE WALKING.—Stretch out along the floor a 12- or 15-foot piece of rope. Now stand on the rope with both feet, toe to heel, and, looking through the large end of a pair of opera glasses or field glasses, walk forward and backward along the rope. If space permits, try a race using two or three ropes.

BALLOON-INFLATING CONTEST.—Supply each player with an ordinary balloon. Instruct the group to inflate their balloons to fullest capacity within 2 minutes. The person who gets his balloon to the largest size within the allotted time is awarded a suitable prize. Many of the participants, in their enthusiasm, will burst their balloons. Others will blow very carefully, fearing that the balloon will explode before the expiration of the time limit. The methods pursued by the strong-lunged contingent and by the overcautious folks will amuse everyone.

SKIN THE SNAKE.—Line up the group in single file. Have each boy stoop over and place his right hand between his legs and grasp the right hand of the boy in front of him with his left hand. When all are ready, the last boy in line should lie on his back while the line moves back over him. The next boy then lies down and so on until every boy is lying down. The last one to lie down then rises to his feet and strides forward, each following in turn, until all are back in their original positions.

BOY-IN-A-BOX MOVIE CAMERA.—For your fair midway, make a large box camera of the "pinhole" type. Folks will gladly line up to get inside. For there they will see pictures form before their very eyes—just like a camera. This is how to make it:

1. Get a large packing carton.
2. Make sure the carton is lightproof. Tape all cracks. Drape a blanket over the entrance. The darker the inside, the clearer your picture will be.
3. Cut a hole about the size of a half dollar in one side. This hole should be slightly above the center so that the boy sitting inside will not block the light entering the hole and passing to the opposite side of the box. Now, paste or tape a piece of black construction paper over this hole and make a pinhole in the center. This pinhole is the lens and works on the same principle as the old box-type camera. You may wish to make a revolving disk of lenses with various-sized holes up to one-eighth of an inch. The brighter the light source and the smaller the lens, the sharper the image.

4. Fasten white paper to the inside of the box on the wall opposite the lens. If you prefer, paint it white. The picture will appear upside down on this screen.

5. Select a bright, sunny day. If indoors, floodlights can be directed on the subject to be projected. Set the box on the ground or on a safe elevated position with its lens toward the subject, which should be from 10 to 20 feet away. The best subject is, of course, a dancing, grimacing Cub Scout who can't wait to get inside and see what makes it tick.

6. Place another Cub Scout in the box. Caution him not to obstruct the lens and to wait until his eyes adjust to the darkness. It helps if he has kept his eyes closed several minutes before entering. If the light source is bright and the box is lightproof, he should see the image on the wall in about a minute. And, it will be an upside-down movie—in color, live! What could be more fun?

1894 TIME TEST.—Ask the audience to stand and remain standing for 49 seconds without looking at a watch or clock. As each person thinks 49 seconds has passed, he or she sits down. Give special notice to anyone who sits down when exactly 49 seconds has passed or comes closest to that time.

WADDLE WALKERS.—Use barrel staves. The idea is to stand on stave with feet about 12 to 15 inches apart. Then, by shifting weight, walk or skid the "waddle" forward. This can be an individual try-your-skill stunt or a race. Staves work best on hard surface.

BETCHA CAN'T.—Try drawing these puzzlers—they're not as easy as they look. Draw each design without crossing a line, retracing a line, starting over, or lifting the pencil from the paper.

BLOCK G PUZZLE.—Enlarge the design shown here and trace it on plywood or heavy cardboard. Cut out, using coping saw or jigsaw if necessary. Make several puzzles so boys can have speed contests.

FOR MORE TRICKS AND PUZZLES.—To find more good tricks and puzzles read:
♦ *Cub Scout Magic*
♦ *Den Chief's Denbook*
♦ *Cub Scout Program Helps*

PART III
ON THE
CUB SCOUT TRAIL

12. THE PACK MEETING

Boys like audiences. They will be frank to tell you that they like to be on display. They like applause. They like attention. They like to feel important. The pack meeting provides all of these things.

It provides a purpose for their play and work. They know that each month there will be a grand climax for all that they are doing in the den. This builds their interest throughout the month. It gives them a definite target and deadline. It gives them a larger experience beyond their own den.

The pack meeting is also one of your best opportunities to interest parents. A well-attended pack meeting shows parents that they belong to a successful organization. Such meetings build an active and enthusiastic parent following, and Cub Scouting fails without that. These, then, are the reasons why the pack meeting is important:

♦ It gives the dens an objective toward which to work.

♦ It builds enthusiasm on the part of boys and parents.

♦ It is the best means of developing parent participation.

♦ It helps the boys to feel that they belong to something larger than their own den.

Your pack will meet one evening each month during the school year, probably in rooms provided by the chartered institution. The Cubmaster will be in charge. During the summer, pack meetings probably will be picnics or other outings during the day. (You'll find more on the summer program in the next chapter.)

You, the assistant Den Mother, and the den chief, probably, with help from the den dad will be in charge of your den during pack meetings. Most of the activities in the pack meeting are done by dens, so your den and the parents of your boys will sit together.

The Cubmaster is responsible for planning the pack meetings. He makes up the agenda at the monthly pack leaders' meeting (explained in the next chapter). It is at this meeting that agreements on program were made after the Cubmaster received from the Den Leader coach (or you and the other Den Mothers) and Webelos den leader a list of your plans for stunts and demonstrations, boys who are to receive advancement awards, and any other ceremonies or events that ought to be included.

Like a den meeting, the pack meeting is divided into fairly distinct parts. Let's look at them.

PART 1—GATHERING PERIOD

Folks never arrive at meetings all at one time. Usually a group gathers over a period of 15 to 20 minutes. At the pack meeting we do not waste this time, but provide interesting things for boys and parents to do. This is important not only from the standpoint of making good use of time, but also to avoid confusion and noise.

WELCOMING COMMITTEE.—Have you ever attended a meeting in a strange place? Did someone go out of his way to welcome you and make you feel at home? If so, you know what an impression it made upon you.

The same thing should happen at your pack meetings. In a way, you are the hostess for your den. Make it a point to welcome your Cubs' parents, especially the mothers. Ask your den dad to serve as a host to the dads of your den. It helps parents feel that the pack meeting is for them. The Cubmaster may ask the 10-year-old Webelos Scouts to serve as ushers or help in welcoming parents in some other way.

DEN EXHIBITS.—At every pack meeting your den should have an exhibit showing what it has accomplished during the month. This provides something interesting for the parents to see while waiting for the meeting to start. It also gives the boys recognition for what they have made. You will find some suggestions on den exhibits at the end of this chapter. This is a fine opportunity to use the assistant Den Mother.

ICEBREAKERS AND GET-ACQUAINTED GAMES.— Sometimes the Cubmaster may use get-acquainted games and stunts to break the ice at pack meetings. You will find some of these in *Cub Scout Program Helps, Group Meeting Sparklers,* and *Games for Cub Scouts.*

Here's a typical icebreaker. As folks arrive, pin on their backs a picture of an object cut from a magazine. Each person must discover the name of the object by asking other folks questions that can be answered by "yes" or "no."

PART 2—MAIN PART OF MEETING

OPENING OR GRAND ENTRANCE.—When the parents and friends have been seated, the Cub Scouts take their places. Seating everybody by dens helps build den spirit and avoids discipline problems. The Cub Scouts may enter with some fanfare in a grand entrance. This is especially good when the boys have made costumes or have projects to show off in connection with the monthly theme or Webelos den activity. The assistant Cubmaster can invite everyone to join in a song, salute to the flag, or try some other appropriate activity.

It's best if both parents and boys can take part in the opening. Sometimes a community sing will get everyone in the right mood.

DEN SKITS AND DEMONSTRATIONS.—The Cubmaster will have scheduled a period for Cub Scout den stunts and Webelos den demonstrations. Now is the time to stage the skit you've been preparing. (See chapter 10.) The Cub Scouts enjoy performing in front of their friends and parents. Parents like this period, too, because they see their own boys in action. The Webelos Scouts will show or demonstrate some project related to the activity badge area they have studied during the month.

No pack meeting would be complete without some thought for audience participation. This is where the *Group Meeting Sparklers* book with its group stunts and mixers can help.

To keep the program moving briskly, there should be very little delay between den stunts and demonstrations. This does not mean, however, that you have to have your den offstage getting ready while another den is performing. Let your boys see the whole show. If your stunt or demonstration is not elaborate, it ought not to take you and the den chief more than a minute to get ready after the previous den has finished. Just make certain that the equipment or costumes needed are ready for immediate use so there will be no delays between stunts.

NEXT MONTH'S PROGRAM.—At each pack meeting the Cubmaster takes a few minutes to explain next month's program to the boys and parents. This gives them something to anticipate.

ACHIEVEMENT AND GRADUATION AWARDS.—Toward the end of each pack meeting, advancement awards are made to the Cub Scouts and Webelos Scouts who have earned them. Although the ceremonies are usually conducted by the Cubmaster, he never presents the awards to the boys alone. Since the parents have helped the boys to earn these awards, it is important that they help present the awards to their own sons. There may also be ceremonies honoring boys or leaders for long service or special training. At the pack leaders' meeting, you will have given the Cubmaster the names of your boys who have earned badges.

Simple ceremonies will be used. Perhaps every 3 or 4 months there will be a more elaborate ceremony to recognize all of the boys who have advanced during that period.

CLOSING.—Usually the closing is quiet and impressive. It is a good idea just before the closing ceremony for the Cubmaster to make last-minute announcements regarding the month ahead.

Following the announcements, the boys and their parents frequently participate in a closing ceremony together. Sometimes they may form a circle and sing a quiet song. Another time both parents and boys may join in a living circle on a den basis only. It is worth considerable effort for the Cubmaster to make the closing ceremony effective and new each month.

ANNUAL PARENTS' MEETING

One pack meeting a year, usually in the early fall, is devoted to explaining Cub Scouting and its aims to the parents. During this parents' meeting, the Cub Scouts are entertained with games, songs, and stories in another room or outside. This is a good time to have a pack uniform inspection rehearsed in which the importance of a uniform and how to wear it can be emphasized. Den chiefs and assistant Cubmasters are usually in charge of the boys.

Communication with parents will be very important to the success of your pack. If the need arises and facilities allow, this idea of having separate meetings of Cub Scouts and parents may be used more than once during the year. A parents' meeting gives the Cubmaster and other pack leaders a chance to show parents how they can cooperate with the pack. The parents might be shown how to use various parts of the advancement program in their own homes. This may be done with dramatizations and demonstrations. Occasionally, a dad who is particularly well qualified in an achievement or elective will demonstrate it.

In addition to a presentation on advancement, there might be a report from the treasurer on the pack budget plan and a statement of financial needs. The Cubmaster can explain how parents can help in the programs for the coming months. He includes an opportunity for parents to ask questions.

THE PACK MEETING AND YOU

You have a definite part in planning all pack meetings. Each month you have an opportunity at the pack leaders' meeting to make suggestions through your Den Leader coach or personally.

PACK MEETING ATTENDANCE.—It is only natural that you will want good attendance of boys and parents at your pack meetings. You will find you won't have much difficulty in getting the boys to attend. If you encourage the boys to get their parents out, you will be surprised at what effective salesmen they can be.

One of your den dad's most important responsibilities is to call all of the dads in his den a few days before the pack meeting. He encourages the dads to attend so that their boys will not be disappointed and embarrassed.

It is a good idea each month if you yourself call the mothers of the boys in your den to encourage their attendance.

PARENT HOSTS.—As suggested in the pack meeting outline, all of the parents of your den are welcomed to the pack meeting. If you are busy with other responsibilities, get a different mother each month to serve as hostess.

DEN EXHIBITS.—There are a few simple rules to keep in mind in connection with your den exhibits at pack meetings. First, arrange them in an orderly fashion. Separate each item carefully from surrounding ones and label it with the name of the maker.

Feature in your exhibit the items related to the theme of the month. Since other Cub Scout dens will be following the same theme, it shows parents the big idea of the month. Of course, you need not limit your exhibit just to the items related to the theme. Advancement items also deserve recognition.

Do not take the entire responsibility for collecting your exhibit, getting it to the pack meeting place, and setting it up. Each parent should see that his son brings his items. Ask the den dad or den chief to arrive at the pack meeting early to help set up.

13. YOUR PROGRAM—WHO PLANS IT

You alone are not expected to find and develop all of the ideas and materials needed to run four lively den meetings each month. If you had to do this without help and also devote an afternoon each week to the leadership of your den meeting, Cub Scouting would become quite a burden.

It is the Cubmaster's responsibility to work with Den Mothers in developing den meeting programs. In most packs, he will have the help of a Den Leader coach who has probably had experience in Cub Scouting and can help you in planning your den meeting programs in detail. The Den Leader coach's duties will be explained in chapter 19, "You and the Den Leader Coach."

Nearly all of the program planning for your den and the whole pack will be done at four meetings.

They are:

1. *Annual Program Planning Conference*
   All pack leaders attend to map out the broad outline for a year's activity.

2. *Monthly Pack Leaders' Meeting*
   All pack leaders except den chiefs attend to make specific program plans for the month ahead. When a pack has a Den Leader coach, the coach may represent the Den Mothers. Den Mothers then attend only if they wish.

3. *Den Mother-Den Leader Coach Meeting*
   The Den Leader coach meets with the Den Mothers to develop specifics for the den meetings. When there is no Den Leader coach, one of the experienced Den Mothers presides.

4. *Den Chiefs' Meeting*
   The Den Mother or Den Leader meets with the den chief once each month to prepare him for the next month's den meetings. The Webelos den chief works directly with his Webelos den leader.

1. ANNUAL PROGRAM PLANNING CONFERENCE

Who attends? All Den Mothers, assistant Den Mothers, Den Leader coach, Webelos den leaders, den chiefs, Cubmaster and assistants, den dads, and other pack committeemen.

What's the purpose? To agree on the program themes and Webelos activity areas to be featured for each of the next 12 months.

When is it held? Spring is best, preferably April.

YOUR PART IN THE MEETING.—Before the annual program planning conference is held, you should talk with the boys of your den. Get them to express themselves about last year's program. Find out what they liked and what they didn't like. Also give them a chance to mention the things which they would like to do during the next 12 months.

At the conference, the things your boys want will be listed on a blackboard or a large piece of wrapping paper. As you and the other pack leaders plan the themes, as many as possible of the boys' ideas should be brought into the program.

At the annual program planning conference in April you will be asked to use your current *Cub Scout Program Helps* so that you will know about the themes and activity badge areas to be covered in the coming year. Your pack will probably choose to use most of these because detailed suggestions and outlines for activities and crafts on them are included month by month in the *Cub Scout Program Helps*. This is mailed directly to you in *Scouting Magazine* each spring.

2. MONTHLY PACK LEADERS' MEETING

Who attends? Den Leader coach, Webelos den leader, den dads and other pack committeemen, Cubmaster and assistants. Den chiefs are not included. Den Mothers and assistant Den Mothers may attend if they wish or if there is no Den Leader coach.

What's the purpose? To make last-minute plans for the forthcoming pack meeting and to plan the highlights of next month's den and pack meetings.

When is it held? Monthly, usually about a week before the regular pack meeting. For this meeting you prepare a Den Advancement Report and give it to your Den Leader coach or Cubmaster.

PACK PROGRAM PLANNING CHART

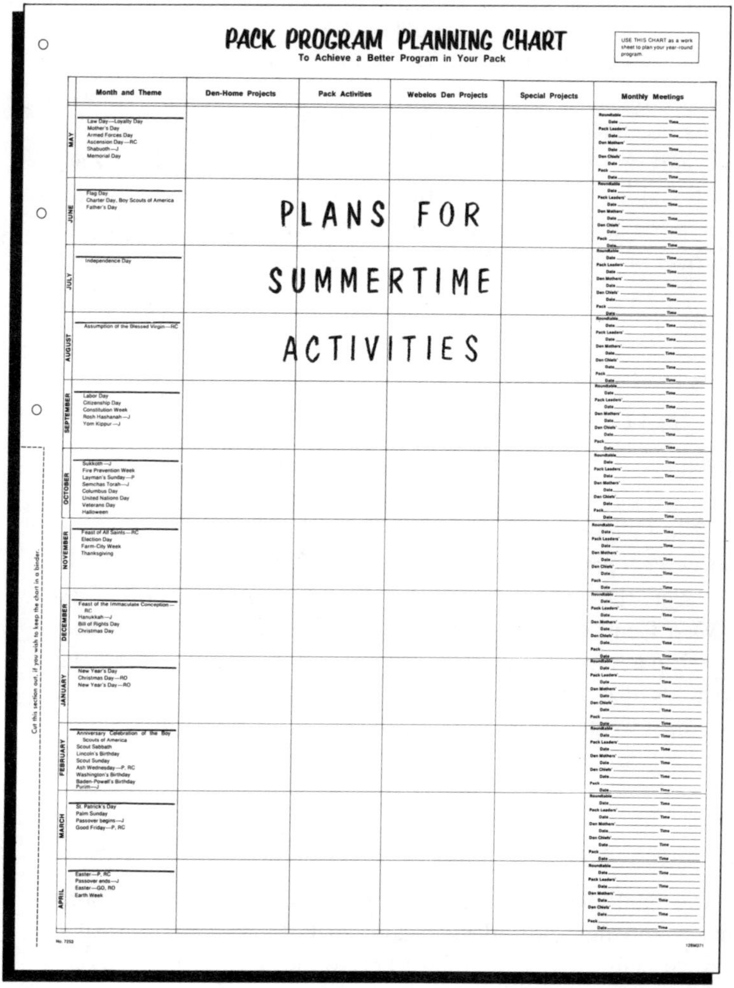

PACK PROGRAM PLANNING CHART

To Achieve a Better Program in Your Pack

USE THIS CHART as a work sheet to plan your year-round program.

	Month and Theme	Den-Home Projects	Pack Activities	Webelos Den Projects	Special Projects	Monthly Meetings
MAY	Law Day—Loyalty Day Mother's Day Armed Forces Day Ascension Day—RC Shabuoth—J Memorial Day					Roundtable ___ Date ___ Time ___ Pack Leaders' ___ Date ___ Time ___ Den Mothers' ___ Date ___ Time ___ Den Chiefs' ___ Date ___ Time ___ Pack ___ Date ___ Time ___
JUNE	Flag Day Charter Day, Boy Scouts of America Father's Day	PLANS FOR				Roundtable ___ Date ___ Time ___ Pack Leaders' ___ Date ___ Time ___ Den Mothers' ___ Date ___ Time ___ Den Chiefs' ___ Date ___ Time ___ Pack ___ Date ___ Time ___
JULY	Independence Day	SUMMERTIME				Roundtable ___ Date ___ Time ___ Pack Leaders' ___ Date ___ Time ___ Den Mothers' ___ Date ___ Time ___ Den Chiefs' ___ Date ___ Time ___ Pack ___ Date ___ Time ___
AUGUST	Assumption of the Blessed Virgin—RC	ACTIVITIES				Roundtable ___ Date ___ Time ___ Pack Leaders' ___ Date ___ Time ___ Den Mothers' ___ Date ___ Time ___ Den Chiefs' ___ Date ___ Time ___ Pack ___ Date ___ Time ___
SEPTEMBER	Labor Day Citizenship Day Constitution Week Rosh Hashanah—J Yom Kippur—J					Roundtable ___ Date ___ Time ___ Pack Leaders' ___ Date ___ Time ___ Den Mothers' ___ Date ___ Time ___ Den Chiefs' ___ Date ___ Time ___ Pack ___ Date ___ Time ___
OCTOBER	Sukkoth—J Fire Prevention Week Layman's Sunday—P Semchas Torah—J Columbus Day United Nations Day Veterans Day Halloween					Roundtable ___ Date ___ Time ___ Pack Leaders' ___ Date ___ Time ___ Den Mothers' ___ Date ___ Time ___ Den Chiefs' ___ Date ___ Time ___ Pack ___ Date ___ Time ___
NOVEMBER	Feast of All Saints—RC Election Day Farm-City Week Thanksgiving					Roundtable ___ Date ___ Time ___ Pack Leaders' ___ Date ___ Time ___ Den Mothers' ___ Date ___ Time ___ Den Chiefs' ___ Date ___ Time ___ Pack ___ Date ___ Time ___
DECEMBER	Feast of the Immaculate Conception—RC Hanukkah—J Bill of Rights Day Christmas Day					Roundtable ___ Date ___ Time ___ Pack Leaders' ___ Date ___ Time ___ Den Mothers' ___ Date ___ Time ___ Den Chiefs' ___ Date ___ Time ___ Pack ___ Date ___ Time ___
JANUARY	New Year's Day Christmas Day—RO New Year's Day—RO					Roundtable ___ Date ___ Time ___ Pack Leaders' ___ Date ___ Time ___ Den Mothers' ___ Date ___ Time ___ Den Chiefs' ___ Date ___ Time ___ Pack ___ Date ___ Time ___
FEBRUARY	Anniversary Celebration of the Boy Scouts of America Scout Sabbath Lincoln's Birthday Scout Sunday Ash Wednesday—P, RC Washington's Birthday Baden-Powell's Birthday Purim—J					Roundtable ___ Date ___ Time ___ Pack Leaders' ___ Date ___ Time ___ Den Mothers' ___ Date ___ Time ___ Den Chiefs' ___ Date ___ Time ___ Pack ___ Date ___ Time ___
MARCH	St. Patrick's Day Palm Sunday Passover begins—J Good Friday—P, RC					Roundtable ___ Date ___ Time ___ Pack Leaders' ___ Date ___ Time ___ Den Mothers' ___ Date ___ Time ___ Den Chiefs' ___ Date ___ Time ___ Pack ___ Date ___ Time ___
APRIL	Easter—P, RC Passover ends—J Easter—GO, RO Earth Week					Roundtable ___ Date ___ Time ___ Pack Leaders' ___ Date ___ Time ___ Den Mothers' ___ Date ___ Time ___ Den Chiefs' ___ Date ___ Time ___ Pack ___ Date ___ Time ___

Cut this section out, if you wish to keep the chart in a binder.

No. 7253

This handy program planning tool is bound into your *Cub Scout Program Helps* annual and is also available as a single chart. Use it as you plan your pack and den programs for the year. Registered leaders will each have one and should fill it out with the information pertaining to their specific needs. Key information on meetings and dates should be duplicated and given to parents following your annual pack program planning conference in April.

In the planning of the month's den programs, the Den Leader coach should be an invaluable help. The Den Leader coach has probably been a Den Mother and has a pretty good idea of activities that work and those that don't. This will put you close to someone who can give some good advice.

The Webelos den leader is concerned mainly with the program planning for the pack meeting. His den of 10-year-old Webelos Scouts does not follow the pack's monthly theme but builds den programs on the 15 Webelos activity areas. These are hobby and vocational interests geared to the abilities of the older Cub Scouts. He reports his plans at the monthly pack leaders' meeting for approval or assistance.

3. DEN MOTHER-DEN LEADER COACH MEETING

Following the monthly pack leaders' meeting, all Den Mothers and assistants meet a day or two later at one of your homes with the Den Leader coach to plan the details of the den meetings. As you work together, you will find yourself looking upon this association as though it were a club. You have a common interest.

Most Den Leaders use the Weekly Den Meeting Program form in their planning. They should use them in this meeting. As details are worked out they should write them on this sheet. This will give them written programs to follow.

4. DEN CHIEFS' MEETING

The final step in den meeting program planning is a conference involving you and your den chief. In this meeting, which may be held in your home just before the start of a new month, review plans for the four meetings ahead using the Weekly Den Meeting Program sheets.

Assign the den chief's duties for each meeting and coach him in the skills he'll need for his part. It is essential that you play up the den chief's role in den leadership and make him feel that he is important in the lives of "his" Cub Scouts.

The Webelos den leader and his Webelos den chief hold similar conferences to work out the details of their weekly programs.

This may be done at a monthly meeting, just before the new month starts, or from week to week.

At this meeting the leader gives the den chiefs a chance to bring up problems or questions.

DOES YOUR PACK OPERATE THIS WAY?

Does your pack plan and prepare for its den and pack programs by using all three of these meetings? The packs which follow this plan usually boast about a successful program that holds boys.

THE SUMMER PROGRAM

Summer is the time for outdoor activities, full of fun and adventure, for both the den and the pack. Help keep your pack going through the summer by encouraging the other leaders to plan a full schedule of activities.

While a challenging summer program requires effort by all leaders, even greater effort is necessary to get going again in the fall if you take a summer break from Cub Scouting. Most important, your Cub Scouts will want to continue during the summer if both the den and pack have exciting things to do.

What should you do in the summer? Well, the possibilities are almost endless. We suggest informal pack meetings and den outings which may or may not relate to the themes for summer.

Pack leaders should remember while planning summer events that themes give the boys new experiences for each month. Summer themes will be found in the current issue of *Cub Scout Program Helps* and *Boys' Life*. For more information refer to *Cub Scout Activities,* No. 4525 and the April, May, June, July, and August issues of *Boys' Life.*

THE DEN IN SUMMER.—Suppose your pack does not plan themes for the summer, but instead schedules various types of trips and outings. What then should your den do?

The first thing to remember is that family activities are perfect for summertime. Here are a few things your den families might do:

♦ Father-and-son picnic, led by the den dad

♦ Father-and-son swimming party

♦ Den parents Fourth of July celebration

♦ Trip to nearby lake or river

♦ Softball games

- Visit to nearby farms or city
- Dad-and-son fishing trip
- Fathers and sons go to a ball game
- Visit to an airport
- Early evening campfire with parents attending
- Family treasure hunt

Most of these events can be handled by you, your assistant, your den dad, and the den chief just as you lead the regular den meetings. Whenever possible, call on parents for help.

THE PACK IN SUMMER.—For the pack, the summer meetings similarly will be outings or trips. If the pack uses themes during the summer, pack activities are pretty well answered. If not, special events are planned, including Webelos den activities, like these:

- Cub Scout and parents' field day, with interden races and contests of all sorts for boys, mothers, and fathers in your pack
- Fourth of July celebration or picnic
- Family treasure hunt
- Airplane model contest
- Day in the Scout council camp (by appointment)
- Trip to a historic site
- A learn-to-swim program

NATIONAL SUMMERTIME PACK AWARD.—The Boy Scouts of America offers the National Summertime Pack Award for packs that hold activities in June, July, and August. Dens averaging at least half of their members at the three summer pack events receive a den participation ribbon for their den flagpole.

Your Cubmaster will have details on this award.

YOUR SUMMER PROGRAM AIDS.—You'll find lots of ideas for your den's summer activities in the following sources:

- Summer themes in *Cub Scout Program Helps*
- *Cub Scout Activities*
- *Cub Scout Water Fun*
- *Den Chief's Denbook*

118

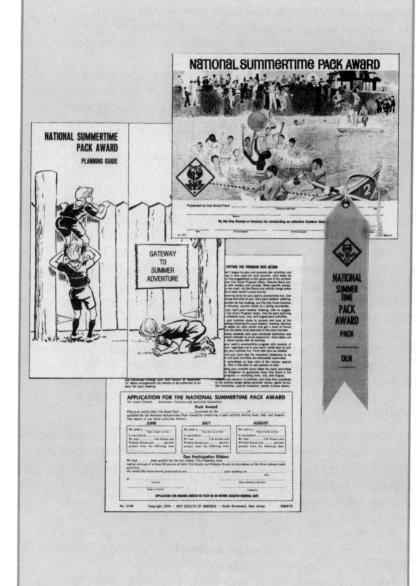

CUB SCOUTING IN THE OUTDOORS

Your boys will probably want to spend as much time as possible outdoors. You will be able to schedule some of your den meetings in a backyard or a public park during much of the year. In some sections of the country, at least the activities part of the den meeting can be held outdoors the year-round.

In most of the country, though, the meetings have to be held indoors through the late fall and winter, but this does not mean there can be no Cub Scout activities outdoors. For example, there might be den father-and-son football trips, den sledding parties, or trips to points of interest.

For special den outings throughout the year, work out the plans with your den dad.

Cub Scouting encourages adventuresome outdoor activities for 8- and 9-year-old boys. These include den picnics, outings, and individual backyard camping. Camping by individual families is consistent with Cub Scouting emphasis upon family activities. Overnight and pack camping are not included because it is felt that these experiences can best be brought to the boy in the Boy Scouting program.

The program for Webelos Scouts in their 10th year may include one or two overnight experiences in which dads participate with their sons. These are individual Webelos den experiences; district or council camping is not permitted for Webelos Scouts.

The point to remember about those den activities that do not include the Cub Scouts' parents is that they should be kept close to home. Backyard events, neighborhood events, activities in a nearby park or playground—this is outdoor Cub Scouting.

COMPETITIVE ACTIVITIES AND SPORTS.—Athletic activity and the contribution a properly balanced program of sports can make in achieving the purposes of Cub Scouting are important. Individual and team sports can be included in your den and pack programs, along with many of the other activities boys enjoy doing.

All competition in Cub Scouting is run on an interden basis within the pack. Do not conduct interpack competitions; avoid overorganization and overemphasis.

Informal competition can help us achieve the goals of Cub Scouting. Competitive games can strengthen a boy's will to win, help him improve his skills, develop him mentally and physically, and teach him the elements of good sportsmanship—win or lose.

Safe swimming can be enjoyed with the family or friends for most of a person's active life. It is a fine, all-round body builder and makes a good summertime den activity.

The Cub Scout Water Fun Book, No. 3220, is full of games designed to help get boys out to the water and learn swimming fundamentals. It contains many helps for safely teaching Cub Scouts how to swim.

Use these rules when swimming on a Cub Scout outing:

♦ First secure a parent approval slip from each boy's parents with a notation on physical condition.

♦ Swimming area shall be safe—a regulated swimming pool or beach or an area that has been checked for safe bottom, proper depth, and absence of dangerous currents. Backyard pools are also to be checked.

♦ Person in charge shall know how to conduct a safe swim including use of the buddy plan where swimmers are paired up to watch one another. In addition, he or she shall either have aquatic safety skills or secure the help of an adult or older Scout with such skills.

♦ When pairing up boys, try to have one older than the other. The recommended standard is for the total age of the pair of buddies to be at least 18 years. The reliability of the plan decreases when the age total is less. To make it work, you may have to use den chiefs or adults as buddies or leaders.

♦ Precautions are worth all our efforts and apparent inconvenience. Following safety recommendations will help prevent the tragedy of a water accident.

For years the Boy Scouts of America has worked to perfect a Safe Swim Defense. The following eight points are guideposts to ensure safe swimming whether with the family, den, or pack:

1. Physical fitness of each participant
2. Qualified supervision
3. Safe swim area
4. Lifeguards on duty
5. A lookout
6. Ability groups
7. Buddy plan
8. Discipline

14. THE OBJECTIVES OF CUB SCOUTING

The objectives of Cub Scouting are something far more than giving boys a good time. The truly big ideas of Cub Scouting are the deeper values that equip boys for a richer and finer life.

It is your responsibility as a Den Mother to interpret these big ideas in such a way that your boys will understand them. No task in Cub Scouting is more important. These ideals are the things which set Cub Scouting apart as something more than a mere recreational activity for boys. They also give a boy a splendid foundation for his Boy Scout experience and a better understanding of the Scout Oath and Law when he learns them later.

It is easy for the ideals of Cub Scouting to become lost in the fun-and-adventure side of the program. It is your opportunity to weave these ideas into your den activities without lecturing or preaching, so that they will come to mean much to your boys.

It is not enough for boys merely to repeat the Cub Scout Promise and the Law of the Pack. No matter how often they repeat the big ideas of Cub Scouting, this does not necessarily guarantee that they understand them. In fact, if they are repeated too often, they may lose their meaning.

One way for you to help your boys get the true meaning of these ideals is occasionally to have a den discussion about them. For example, ask your boys what they think it means to be square. How far must one go to meet that obligation? Should one be square to another person who, in turn, is not also square? Remind them that the Cub Scout badges are square because this reminds Cub Scouts to be square.

Ask your boys at some den meeting how they can tell when they have really done their best? How good is a person's best? How can they be sure that they cannot do better?

If you were to have such discussions too often, they would become tiresome. However, you can do it safely at least twice a year, and the boys will gain by the experience.

You can also remind them of these big ideas by keeping them aware of the Cub Scout sign and the Cub Scout salute. Work these things into ceremonies occasionally, but try to avoid preaching.

Help your boys understand that it takes a brave man to always be square and always do his best. There is nothing childish about those ideas.

CUB SCOUTING'S IDEALS

THE CUB SCOUT PROMISE

The Promise is written in boy language, short and simple, so every boy of Cub Scout age can grasp its meaning.

"Be square" is one of the key points in the Promise. Help your boys to see that it is not always easy to be fair to the other fellow. Sometimes fairness requires unselfishness and placing himself second to someone else. To "be square" the Cub Scout must treat other people as he would like them to treat him.

THE LAW OF THE PACK

The Cub Scout follows Akela.—In Cub Scouting the word Akela *(pronounced Ah-kay'-lah)* means "good leader." To a Cub Scout, Akela is his mother or father, his teacher, his Cubmaster, his Den Mother, or his den chief. Akela is anyone who has shown that he or she is able and willing to be a good leader for the Cub Scouts to follow. (See "Story of Akela," *Wolf Cub Scout Book.*)

Another point to stress here is the fact that in order to be a good leader one must first learn to be a good follower. So the key in the first part of the Law of the Pack is "follows."

The Cub Scout helps the pack go.—When a boy becomes 8 years old, he is beginning to realize that his wishes and desires are not the only things for him to consider. Cub Scouting may give him his first experience as a member of an organized group. That means he is taking on a new obligation. He is no longer just a boy, but a member of a den and a pack. He can "help the pack go" by being a loyal Cub Scout, by attending all meetings, by following his leader, and by making his pack better because he is a member. The key word in this portion of the Law is helps.

The pack helps the Cub Scout grow.—This part of the Law of the Pack helps the Cub Scout to see that, in meeting his obligations to other people, he brings more fun and satisfaction to himself. He helps the pack go, and in return the pack helps the Cub Scout grow—grow in fun and in spirit. Here the key word is helps.

124

CUB SCOUT PROMISE

I,_____ , promise

To do my best

To do my duty

To God and my country,

To be square, and

To obey the Law of the Pack.

THE LAW OF THE PACK

The Cub Scout follows Akela.

The Cub Scout helps the pack go.

The pack helps the Cub Scout grow.

The Cub Scout gives goodwill.

The Cub Scout gives goodwill.—It's a great feeling that comes to the boy when he does well those things which his parents and leaders expect him to do. It's even a greater feeling when he does more than he is actually expected to do. Through this part of the Law of the Pack the boy becomes conscious of the pleasure of doing things for other people.

Help him to develop the habit of looking for ways to make other people happy. Don't expect too much. He is only 8 or 9 years old. But a word of encouragement from you at a time when he has undertaken some goodwill project will speed him on to further effort. Help him to see that one of the things that makes a person happy is the desire to go out of his way to help other people. The key word here is gives. So three key words of Cub Scouting are follows, helps, and gives.

CUB SCOUT SIGN.—The Cub Scout sign is made with the right hand held high and straight up above the shoulder, the fingers held as shown in the illustration on page 123.

The two extended fingers stand for "be square" and "obey" in the Cub Scout Promise. They also stand for the two alert ears of the Wolf. Your boys will enjoy knowing that this is the sign of Cub Scouts all over the world. The sign is used when repeating the Cub Scout Promise, in the living circle, and in other ceremonies. It can also be used as a sign of greeting from one Cub Scout to another.

CUB SCOUT HANDSHAKE.—The Cub Scout handshake is done with the right hand, with the first two fingers along the side of the other person's wrist. This handshake is used by Cub Scouts and Cub Scout leaders everywhere. The meaning of the handshake is that those making it are square and obey the Law of the Pack. The handshake is illustrated on page 123.

CUB SCOUT MOTTO.—"Do Your Best" is the Cub Scout motto. It is one of the most important things for the boy of Cub Scout age to learn. Often he becomes so interested in beating the other fellow that he fails to see that the important thing is to do the best he can at everything.

One boy's best might be quite different from another boy's best. Help your boys to see that no one can find fault with them if they always do their best in everything they tackle.

CUB SCOUT SALUTE.—In giving the Cub Scout salute, the hand is held as it is in giving the Cub Scout sign, except that the first two fingers are closed together. The salute is used in flag ceremonies and as a means of showing respect to den and pack leaders. It is illustrated on page 123.

LIVING CIRCLE.—This is an important Cub Scout ceremony that may be used occasionally as an opening or closing for a den or pack meeting. It reminds the boy of the friendships he is making and links him with all other Cub Scouts in the tribe of the Webelos.

Cub Scouts (and leaders) face inward in a close circle. They turn slightly to the right and extend left hands into the circle. Each thumb is pointed to the right, and each person grasps the thumb of the person on his left. With the right hand, each boy gives the Cub Scout sign. The Promise, Law of the Pack, or motto can then be repeated. The circle is shown on page 123.

The living circle can be elaborated by moving all the left hands up and down in a pumping motion while the Cub Scouts say *"Ah-h—kay-y—la! We-e-e'll do-o-o ou-u-r best!"*—snapping into individual salutes at the word "best."

CUB SCOUT CODE.—The secret code of the Cub Scout is a message written with the letters of the words reversed, as follows: *A buc tuocs si riaf.*—A Cub Scout is fair.

WEBELOS.—Webelos is a coined word with an Indian sound which has these meanings for Cub Scouts:

1. Webelos is the highest rank in Cub Scouting, the last step before a boy enters Boy Scouting.
2. The word Webelos has a secret meaning because it is formed from the phrase: We'll be loyal Scouts. This reminds Cub Scouts that they will someday be Boy Scouts. The word is pronounced *Wee'-buh-lows*.

15. THE ADVANCEMENT PLAN

There are certain things the average American boy is going to do whether anyone encourages him or not. These things are just part of most boys.

He's going to play games, he's probably going to collect things, and most likely he'll enjoy making things.

The Cub Scout advancement plan recognizes boys' natural urges. It encourages boys to give expression to them by learning how to do them better.

Many of the achievements and electives your boys will be called upon to do to advance in rank are this type of activity—the things he will do in any case. For example, in the Wolf rank, the Feats of Skill achievement asks him to climb a tree, learn to fall properly, and play catch. To most boys, this sort of activity is as natural as breathing. In other Wolf achievements, your 8-year-olds will learn how to care for and use a knife safely, and how to keep their collections in an orderly way. Again, these are things that your Cub Scouts will take to with great interest, simply because they are things they want to do.

BUT . . .

There are some things that boys must learn that do not come so naturally. Every boy finds himself involved in constant conflict between the things he wants to do and the things he must do. But that's life. It will help him to learn that lesson at Cub Scout age. The advancement plan makes learning less painful.

As he progresses through the achievements and electives, the boy is expected to learn about his flag; to help at home, in school, and in church; to learn the rules of cleanliness; and to learn to be helpful to people through knowledge of his community. If the parents approach these things in the wrong way, they are quite likely to smother the fun of Cub Scouting. That is the test of the

advancement plan—whether we can get boys to do these less natural things without serious resentment.

This leads us to your relationship as a Den Mother to Cub Scout advancement.

YOUR RESPONSIBILITIES

You have three responsibilities in connection with advancement. First, to stimulate interest in advancement. While boys actually pass their achievements and electives to their parents, you and your den chief should help the Cub Scouts to prepare themselves to pass them. Your den chief can be especially helpful by giving boys a chance to point out their problems and then giving them a hand. This can be done in an interesting manner through use of playways. You will find sample playways in this book and more on pages 61-73 of the *Den Chief's Denbook.*

Your second responsibility is to help parents understand the plan and use it intelligently. Your close contact with the boys places you in a position to be especially helpful.

Be familiar with the parent supplements in the Wolf and Bear books. These are designed to guide parents in using the advancement plan with their sons.

Finally, your third responsibility is to keep a record of the achievements and electives completed by your Cub Scouts. Each month, at the pack leaders' meeting, your Den Advancement Report should be submitted to the Cubmaster or his assistant listing the names of the boys in your den who have earned badges and arrow points. The Den Leader coach may transmit this report for you. A well-kept record will avoid delay in recognition of your boys. The Cubmaster will obtain the badges your boys have earned from the local council office and plan for an appropriate ceremony at the next pack meeting.

HOW THE ADVANCEMENT PLAN WORKS

There are four ranks in Cub Scouting, all but one of them geared to the boy's age. The exception is the first rank—Bobcat. All Cub Scouts (including 10-year-olds) must pass the Bobcat requirements before starting on the rank for their age.

There are five simple requirements:
1. Learn and give the Cub Scout Promise.
2. Say the Law of the Pack. Tell what it means.

130

3. Tell what Webelos means.
4. Show the Cub Scout sign and handshake. Tell what they mean.
5. Give the Cub Scout motto and salute. Tell what they mean.

The boy studies these, and when his parents feel he has learned them, they will inform you so that he can get his Bobcat pin. He wears this metal pin centered on his left pocket until he has earned a higher rank. Then he must remove it.

If he is 8 (or in the third grade), the new Cub Scout begins work on the Wolf achievements as soon as he has earned the Bobcat pin. There are 12 of them, all well within the ability of a normal 8-year-old. His parents must approve his work on each achievement by signing his book. The boy brings the book to a den meeting after they have signed so that you can keep a record of his progress on the Cub Scout Advancement Chart.

When he has passed all 12 achievements to the satisfaction of his parents, he has earned the Wolf badge, and you report this to the Cubmaster. After he gets the Wolf badge, he may explore any of 20 elective activity areas in his Wolf book. These are mostly hobby interests that will open up new worlds of fun for the boy. In each of the electives, the Cub Scout elects to work on certain projects. When the boy has completed 10 projects, he receives a Gold Arrow Point that is worn under his Wolf badge. For each 10 additional projects completed, he gets a Silver Arrow Point. You keep a record of the projects on the wall chart and on his advancement record sheet. When a boy is entitled to an arrow point, inform the Cubmaster by listing him on the Den Advancement Report.

The boy may pick and choose as he likes among the electives. When properly guided, he explores many challenging fields.

While there is no limit to the number of arrow points a boy may earn, it is unwise to stimulate him to the extent that the number becomes more important than the fun he is having.

REPEATING PROJECTS

If you will turn to the Secret Codes elective in the *Wolf Cub Scout Book,* you will find after the requirement for the first project the words, "Each time you do this differently, it counts as a completed project." The words mean exactly what they say. Every time the boy thinks up and uses a different secret code, he moves a step closer toward an arrow point.

The reason for this is that we want to give the boy the privilege of exploring any field in which he is especially interested. Such an experience may lead him toward a lifetime hobby. However, it is of the utmost importance for you to help parents understand that when a boy begins to repeat a project, that's the time for the parents to become more strict.

For example, turn to the Model Boats elective in the *Wolf Cub Scout Book*. Let's assume that Jimmy chooses to pass an elective requirement in project 2—Make or put together a model of some well-known type of boat. He completes the requirement and receives his credit toward an arrow point. He enjoys the experience so much that he decides he would like to make another model, and this is another of the projects which can be repeated for credit. It is up to the parents at that point to see that the boy makes a better boat than the last one he made. They should guide their son so that he will not merely throw together many boats just to pass requirements toward another arrow point.

In both the Wolf and Bear years, there are only a few electives like these in which a boy can do a project more than once. There are four multiple elective projects in the Wolf Book—Electives:

1. Secret Codes   3. Handicraft
5. Model Boats   9. Parties and Gifts

and four projects in the Bear book—Electives:

6. Aircraft   13. Magic
14. Landscaping   16. Repairs

FROM WOLF TO BEAR

When the Cub Scout reaches his ninth birthday, he leaves the Wolf program and begins work on the Bear achievements. However, if one of your Cub Scouts has not quite completed the Wolf achievements by his ninth birthday, he should be given a few extra weeks to finish them so that he can earn the Wolf badge before going on to Bear.

There are 12 achievements and 20 electives in the Bear year also, and the procedure is almost exactly the same. In only one respect is it different. When a boy has earned the Bear badge, he may work on electives in either the Wolf or the Bear books to complete projects for arrow points he will wear under his Bear badge. As you did in his Wolf year, you keep a record of his achievements and elective credits and inform the Cubmaster when the boy has earned a badge or arrow point.

If a boy joins Cub Scouts when he is nine, he first earns the Bobcat pin. He then begins work on the Bear achievements.

FROM BEAR TO WEBELOS

At 10, a Cub Scout may transfer into the Webelos den, which includes all the boys of that age in your pack. It is possible that some of your boys may be reluctant to leave your den, because they are slow to advance or are backward or shy. Encourage them to make the big step into the Webelos den where they can be with the pack's older boys and enjoy the excitement and adventure that leads to Boy Scouting. The Cubmaster and Webelos den leader can help attract boys to the Webelos den as they near their 10th birthday, and no doubt they will do so by talking about it at pack meetings.

Make sure that the transfer from your den to the Webelos den is recognized with a suitable ceremony in the pack and a simpler one in the den.

To understand fully how the advancement plan works and to see what is required of the Cub Scouts, be sure to look over the Wolf and Bear books. Incidentally, they contain excellent craft projects and ideas that you can tie into your theme program!

THE PARENTS AND ADVANCEMENT

The advancement plan brings Cub Scouting directly into the home. It's a boy-parent experience. More particularly, it's a dad-and-son experience, because it's the dad more than the mother who needs to have a closer relationship with his son. Through doing together, dad and son get to know each other better.

Suggest to each new parent that after removing and reading the parents' supplement in their boy's Cub Scout book that they review the book by going over it page by page.

You can help parents by pointing out to them ways to make achievements the result of natural family experience. By way of example, let's look for a minute at the Family Fun achievement for the Wolf rank. The boy must do two of the following: make a homemade game and play it with his family, plan and go on a family walk or picnic, or read together with his family.

One approach would be for dad or mother to suggest that these be done merely to pass the achievement. A better approach would be for dad to suggest a walk in the woods or the nearest park to see who can find the most birds, and to organize a family game night or reading night. After the boy has enjoyed the experiences, dad can surprise him by signing for his achievement.

DOING FOR THE FUN OF DOING

The most important thing for parents to learn is that the emphasis is on doing—not getting. The experience is the important thing—not the badge. Most achievement and elective projects may be approached on this basis. They are fun in themselves. The only reason for having the badge is that a boy desires recognition for what he does. If parents are not careful, the badge can be overemphasized so the boy loses interest in the activity itself.

HOW STRICT SHOULD THE PARENT BE?

One of the things you must help parents think through is the need for a happy balance between expecting too much and expecting too little in achievements and electives. Often dad's tendency is to measure his son's efforts with an adult yardstick. If we are too critical in our approach, the boy is likely to lose confidence. Since success is important to him, the loss of confidence often brings an equal loss of interest in Cub Scouting.

On the other hand, some parents are inclined to be too easy on their boys. This may result from an overanxiety to see that their sons achieve recognition. Sometimes it occurs because of lack of interest on the part of parents; after all, the easiest way is to sign the book when the boy asks the parents to do so!

You can help parents in this problem by pointing out to them the value of interesting the boy in beating his own record. He should always be encouraged to do his best. That is the measurement in Cub Scouting—not whether he does better than the boy next door, but whether he does the best he himself can do, and whether he does something better than before.

Letting the boy get by too easily teaches him to avoid the rules of the game. He may experiment with his parents to see whether he can get by with something that may not quite meet the requirements. If parents let him do so, great damage can be done. That is influencing character in the wrong direction, and no thoughtful parents want to be a part of such a process.

The key to the happy medium on this question of how much the parents should expect remains the Cub Scout motto, "Do your best."

WHAT CAN YOU DO ABOUT IT?

What if a boy comes to your den meeting with many achievements signed in his book since the last den meeting? You are quite certain that he could not master that many achievements thoroughly in so short a time. Should you refuse to give him credit? Should you require him to pass them over again to you?

No! Once the parent has signed the boy's book, you have no right to refuse to recognize the signature. However, you have an obligation to make certain that the parents understand the advancement plan.

This must be done tactfully, because success depends upon the goodwill of the parent. One good way to get at this problem is by dropping in to see the boy's mother. It's surprising how much you can do through asking questions.

Here are some typical ones: Are you having an interesting time with your boy in connection with the advancement plan? Do you find it hard to use the advancement plan as a basis for natural family activity? Do you find it difficult to get him to do a thorough job on his achievements? Are there any questions I can answer? How can I help you to use the advancement plan as effectively as you would like to use it?

Here is another tip that may help you in dealing with parents in such a situation. Rather than mentioning the specific problem, approach them as though it were a routine contact from you. You'll find folks a lot more agreeable if you always approach them on the basis of wanting to help them. That's disarming, especially when your only motive is on behalf of their own son.

Of course, the best time to deal with such problems is before they happen. Have a frank discussion with parents before boys become members of your den. Point out the dangers of expecting too much or too little. Also try to have a parents' meeting for your den early in the fall season, with the advancement plan as a subject for discussion. Use the parent supplements in the Wolf and Bear books as source material. Perhaps the Cubmaster or the advancement man on the pack committee may help you make a presentation on the values inherent in Cub Scout advancement and how parents can use the plan wisely.

In some dens Cub Scouts are asked to bring to den meetings projects they have completed for those achievements in which something is made. These projects are shown at pack meetings. This den policy helps cut down the number of unearned signatures for achievements and electives.

HOW FAST SHOULD A BOY ADVANCE?

Naturally, the most important thing is to see that each boy earns the badge of rank for his age.

Parents should not be encouraged to rush their boys through the 12 required achievements of each rank. Normally, it should take a boy about 6 months to complete the required achievements for any rank. There is no rule about it, but if he is rushed too rapidly, it may be difficult to hold his interest with the electives through the rest of the year. This is important because he cannot begin to work on the achievements for the next rank until he has reached the age required for that rank.

Mother and dad must help their son find his own rate of advancement. Pressure is almost always unwise. The important thing is for the 8-year-old, for example, to complete his Wolf achievements so that he has a chance to earn one or two arrow points before he becomes 9.

THE CUB SCOUT ADVANCEMENT CHART

You'll find the Cub Scout Advancement Chart (shown on page 145) most helpful. Ask your den dad to mount the chart on plywood or composition board to make it easier for you to display and handle.

At each den meeting you can use the advancement chart in a little ceremony. When a boy has completed an achievement, allow him to come forward and color in or date the achievement he has completed. Any boy who has completed an elective credit may be asked to come forward and color in the appropriate section on the chart after you have dated it.

When a Cub Scout transfers to the Webelos den, you may want to cut his individual chart from the large wall chart, frame it, and present it to him. Replacements for the Cub Scout Advancement Chart may be secured from your local Scout distributor.

Take your den chart to every pack meeting and put it on display as a part of your den exhibit. This allows parents to see how their boys are progressing.

DEN DOODLES

The den doodle is a clever way of recording advancement of the boys in your den. You will find some illustrations of typical den doodles in chapter 3.

Usually the den doodle is topped by a totem of a figure chosen by the den for its symbol. Under the totem is space for each boy to hang his advancement record. For example, your den might use spools to denote advancement. Red spools might denote Wolf achievements; and blue spools, Bear. Each time a boy completes an achievement he paints a spool the correct color and ties it to his string on the den doodle.

Den doodles are limited only by the imagination of the Den Mother, den chief, and boys who create them. Give your boys an opportunity to think up their own original den doodle.

16. YOUR DEN RECORDS AND FINANCES

You have plenty to do as a Den Mother without added worries about complicated records or finances. Just a few simple records are necessary for your den. Most of the pack's records will be kept by other pack leaders.

As to finances, your only regular chore is collecting the boys' dues at each den meeting. However, you should be aware of how your pack is financed, and also how your den can earn extra money if it is needed.

This chapter is in two sections. The first deals with den records; the second, with finances.

First the records.

DEN RECORD.—The Cub Scout Den Record is a form which you will find very helpful. It gives you a place to record all the information you need and is made to fit into a loose-leaf notebook. You need only one of these forms for your den.

The roster side of the form includes a place to record each advancement in rank. On the reverse side is sufficient space to keep an attendance and dues record for the entire year. It is likely that your Boy Scout office will have this form.

DEN ADVANCEMENT REPORT.—At the close of the third meeting of the month, the Den Mother and den chief record Cub Scout advancement on this form, and transmit this report to the Cubmaster at the pack leaders' meeting. The Den Leader coach may do this for each Den Mother.

DEN DUES ENVELOPES.—You will find it best to collect the weekly dues at each den meeting. Either the Weekly Den Dues Envelope or the Monthly Den Dues Envelope is handy for keeping the money. Space is provided for listing the names of boys and the amounts paid. Fill in the date of your den meeting, write your name on the envelope, seal it, and give to your Den Leader

coach or to the pack treasurer at the monthly pack leaders' meeting. He will tear off the receipt tab for your record.

Any other plan makes it difficult to handle pack finances in a businesslike manner.

CUB SCOUT ADVANCEMENT CHART.—In addition to the advancement record which you can keep on the Den Record sheet, you will want to use the Cub Scout Advancement Chart. The chart keeps before your den the record of each boy and the progress he is making. The chart is colorful and will add a decorative effect to your den meeting place. As boys transfer into the Webelos den, their individual advancement record can be cut from the chart and replaced with another from a pad of 25 replacement charts.

INDIVIDUAL CUB SCOUT RECORD.—Many Den Mothers like to keep an Individual Cub Scout Record sheet for each boy in their den. It gives them space for recording a boy's advancement and attendance.

When one of your Cub Scouts becomes 10 and goes into the Webelos den, his records should go with him. Be sure the Webelos den leader gets his advancement and dues records.

YOUR DEN FINANCES

Cub Scouting is one program in which a great deal is done without the expenditure of large sums of money. But Cub Scouting cannot exist without any funds at all.

Where does the money come from? There are four sources:

1. *The boy and his parents*—Each of your Cub Scouts pays a small weekly amount as dues.

2. *The pack*—The boys' dues are the chief income for the pack. The pack committee and pack leaders draw up a budget based primarily upon income from dues, and all regular expenses are paid from these funds. For that reason, all dues you collect must be turned in to the pack treasury.

3. *The chartered institution*—By providing a meeting place, with its necessary maintenance and utilities, the institution that sponsors your pack helps with the costs. The institution may also help by establishing the revolving fund in the pack's budget. The revolving fund is used to meet immediate needs but is replaced later for other unexpected expenditures.

4. *The community*—Your town supports Cub Scouting by giving money to the local council and the services it provides through united funds, sustaining memberships, bequests, and contributions to the council.

EARNING MONEY

The pack's budget probably will cover all the necessary expenses of Cub Scouting, including such items as reregistering the boys each year, subscriptions to *Boys' Life* magazine, goodwill fund, badges and insignia, and perhaps new Cub Scout books. You and the other pack leaders will decide what to include.

What if your pack or den wants additional funds for special equipment or pack or den flags—items which are not included in the pack budget?

The pack will earn the money needed, making sure that the project is compatible with the aims and ideals of Cub Scouting. The committee will consider the project in the light of Scouting's policies on money earning. These are summarized on the back of the Unit Money-Earning Application form, which provides a place for the local council's stamp of approval. There you will find 10 guides that are helpful in determining whether a money-earning project is good for the den and pack, good for the community, and good for Scouting. Let them be your standards.

CUB SCOUT DEN RECORD

DEN NO. _____ PACK NO. _____ DEN MEETINGS HELD _____ DAY _____ TIME _____ PLACE _____

DEN CHIEF

NAME _____

ADDRESS _____

PHONE _____ TROOP NO. _____ RANK _____

DEN MOTHER

NAME _____

ADDRESS _____

PHONE _____

DEN DAD

NAME _____

ADDRESS _____

HOME PHONE _____ BUSINESS PHONE _____

NAME AND ADDRESS	PHONE	Birth Date	School Grade	Became Cub Scout	Date Will Become 10	Bobcat	Wolf	Gold Arrow	Silver Arrow	Silver Arrow	Silver Arrow	Bear	Gold Arrow	Silver Arrow	Silver Arrow	Silver Arrow	Joined Webelos Den
D – Denner AD – Asst. Denner																	

HOW TO USE THIS FORM

| D | GEORGE OLSEN, 65 MARKHAM ST. | CO-5-2214 | 7/57 | 8/65 | 1/58 | 9/65 | 12/65 | 10/65 | 1/66 | 7/66 | 8/66 | 9/66 | 7/67 | 8/67 | 10/67 | 1/68 | 4/68 | 8/68 |

DEN MOTHERS, this is your permanent record of each Cub Scout from the time he joins the den until he transfers, goes into a Webelos den, or becomes a Boy Scout. Indicate dates of advancement, as shown above, i.e., month and year, thus 5/47. As new boys join, fill in their names, etc. When a boy leaves the den, draw a line through his name. Use a second form when this one is filled.

DEN ADVANCEMENT REPORT

DEN _____ PACK _____ DATE _____

NOTE TO THE LEADERS OF CUB SCOUT DENS AND WEBELOS DENS—Before submitting this record, make certain that full and correct information for each Cub Scout or Webelos Scout is given, and that he is actually a registered member of your pack and is qualified as to age to receive the advancement in rank indicated. Fill out this form at the end of your third den meeting and take it to the pack leaders' meeting where a composite request will be made for the entire pack.

BOYS' NAMES	AWARDS				ARROW POINTS*		ACTIVITY BADGES																		
	BOBCAT	WOLF	BEAR	WEBELOS	GOLD	SILVER	AQUANAUT	ARTIST	ATHLETE	CITIZEN	CRAFTSMAN	ENGINEER	FORESTER	GEOLOGIST	NATURALIST	OUTDOORSMAN	SCHOLAR	SCIENTIST	SHOWMAN	SPORTSMAN	TRAVELER	CUB SCOUT GRADUATION CERTIFICATE	SERVICE STAR**
(CHECK MARK [√] INDICATES RECOGNITION DESIRED)																								
*Designate arrow points by rank. (W) Wolf. (B) Bear.																								
**Designate proper service star (year pin) by number of years.																								

The above members of my den have completed requirements for badges indicated. These awards should be available for presentation at our next pack meeting. Use space on the back to report boy problems: not advancing, not paying dues, not wearing uniform, poor attendance, discipline, inactive, etc.

_____
Den Mother
or
Webelos Den Leader

BOY SCOUTS OF AMERICA

DEN MOTHER OR DEN LEADER _____ DEN _____ PACK _____ MONTH _____			
NAME	DEN MEETING ATTENDANCE	DUES PAID	UNIFORM WORN
TOTALS			

These dues cover the fo...
and Awards ● Handicra...

WEEKLY DEN DUES ENVELOPE

Record of Den No. _____ Pack _____

Name	Present	Uniform Worn	Dues Paid	
TOTALS				

Date of Meeting _____ Den Leader _____

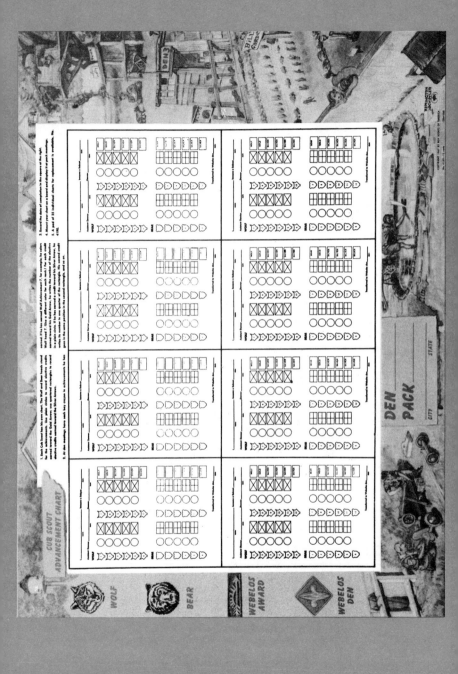

No. 3827
1MM667

INDIVIDUAL CUB SCOUT RECORD

Pack No._____ Den No._____

PERSONAL DATA

Name _____

Address _____

City_____State and ZIP_____

Home phone_____Date of birth_____

Church or synagogue_____

School _____

_____

Parent's name _____

Business address _____

City_____State and ZIP_____

Business phone_____ Occupation_____

MEMBERSHIP

DATE

Became Cub Scout (registered)..........._____

Joined Webelos den...................._____

Transferred into pack................._____

Transferred out of pack..............._____

Became Boy Scout (registered).........._____

Dropped from pack...................._____

Tenure when separated

Less than 1 year....... 1 to 2 years.......

2 to 3 years.......

LEADERSHIP

	FROM	TO
Denner..............	_____	_____
Assistant denner.........	_____	_____

ATTENDANCE AND DUES

D = Present at den meeting
P = Present at pack meeting
M_1 = One parent present at pack meeting
M_2 = Two parents present at pack meeting

S = Present at special pack activity
5, 10, 25 = Amount paid on date shown (dues)
√ = Dues paid ahead or back

YEAR	ATTENDANCE	DUES	YEAR	ATTENDANCE	DUES	YEAR	ATTENDANCE	DUES
DATE → JAN.			DATE → JAN.			DATE → JAN		
DATE → FEB.			DATE → FEB.			DATE → FEB		
DATE → MAR.			DATE → MAR.			DATE → MAR.		
DATE → APR.			DATE → APR.			DATE → APR		
DATE → MAY			DATE → MAY			DATE → MAY		
DATE → JUNE			DATE → JUNE			DATE → JUNE		
DATE → JULY			DATE → JULY			DATE → JULY		
DATE → AUG.			DATE → AUG.			DATE → AUG.		
DATE → SEPT			DATE → SEPT.			DATE → SEPT.		
DATE → OCT			DATE → OCT.			DATE → OCT.		
DATE → NOV.			DATE → NOV.			DATE → NOV.		
DATE → DEC.			DATE → DEC.			DATE → DEC.		

BUDGET: The boys' dues collected should cover the following items in the pack budget: Registration, *Boys' Life*, Badges and Insignia, Program Material, New Cub Scout Book, Goodwill Fund, Reserve Fund.

BOY SCOUTS OF AMERICA

ADVANCEMENT RECORD

This Cub Scout becomes 10 on _____ (Date)

and will be eligible to join a Webelos den.

BOBCAT
1. Learn and take the Cub Scout Promise . . . _____ __
2. Repeat and explain the Law of the Pack . . . _____
3. Explain the meaning of Webelos . . . . ._____
4. Show and explain the Cub Scout sign and
   handclasp . . . . ._____
5. Explain and give the Cub Scout motto
   and salute . . . . ._____

BOBCAT BADGE AWARDED . . . . (Date) _____

HOW TO USE THIS FORM:
For ranks of Bobcat, Wolf, Bear, arrow points, Webelos activity badges, and Webelos Award, the entries should consist of the date (i.e., month and year). For recording the starred electives a "tally" system may be used since some of these electives may be done more than once. A tally entry (I) is given for each time the elective project is completed. Four individual tally entries with a diagonal line across them equals 5 thus: ⟋⟋⟋⟋

WOLF ACHIEVEMENTS
1. Feats of Skill . . . . _____
2. Flag . . . . _____
3. Keeping Healthy . . . . _____
4. Your Home and Community . _____
5. Whittling . . . . _____
6. Collections . . . . _____
7. Conservation . . . . _____
8. Tying Things . . . . _____
9. Home Safety . . . . _____
10. Family Fun . . . . _____
11. Religious Activities . . . . . . _____
12. Books . . . . _____
BADGE AWARDED . . . .(date) _____

WOLF ELECTIVES
1. *Secret Codes . . . . _____
2. Dramatics . . . . _____
3. *Handicraft . . . . _____
4. Baseball . . . . _____
5. *Model Boats . . . . _____
6. Kites . . . . _____
7. Foot Power . . . . _____
8. Machinery . . . . _____
9. *Parties and Gifts . . . . _____
10. Indians . . . . _____
11. Songs . . . . _____
12. Drawing . . . . _____
13. Birds . . . . _____
14. Pets . . . . _____
15. Gardening . . . . _____
16. Water and Soil Conservation _____
17. Cooking . . . . _____
18. Outing . . . . _____
19. Fishing . . . . _____
20. Sports . . . . _____
GOLD ARROW POINT . . . . _____
SILVER ARROW POINT . . . . . . _____
SILVER ARROW POINT . . . . . . _____

BEAR ACHIEVEMENTS
1. Wildlife Conservation . . . . . _____
2. Woodworking . . . . _____
3. Using Rope . . . . _____
4. Outdoor Games . . . . _____
5. Traffic Safety . . . . _____
6. American Heritage . . . . _____
7. Family Get-Together . . . . . . _____
8. Cub Scout Fitness . . . . _____
9. Writing . . . . _____
10. American Folklore . . . . _____
11. Religious Activities . . . . . . _____
12. Protection . . . . _____
BADGE AWARDED . . . .(date) _____

BEAR ELECTIVES
1. Skies . . . . _____
2. Weather . . . . _____
3. Radio . . . . _____
4. Electricity . . . . _____
5. Big Boats . . . . _____
6. *Aircraft . . . . _____
7. Things That Go . . . . _____
8. Bicycling . . . . _____
9. Cub Scout Band . . . . _____
10. Masks . . . . _____
11. Photography . . . . _____
12. Nature Crafts . . . . _____
13. *Magic . . . . _____
14. Landscaping . . . . _____
15. Farm Animals . . . . _____
16. *Repairs . . . . _____
17. Backyard Gym . . . . _____
18. Swimming . . . . _____
19. Family Alert . . . . _____
20. Sports . . . . _____
GOLD ARROW POINT . . . . _____
SILVER ARROW POINT . . . . . . _____
SILVER ARROW POINT . . . . . . _____

WEBELOS SCOUT ACTIVITY BADGES
1. Aquanaut . . . . _____
2. Artist . . . . _____
3. Athlete . . . . _____
4. Citizen . . . . _____
5. Craftsman . . . . _____
6. Engineer . . . . _____
7. Forester . . . . _____
8. Geologist . . . . _____
9. Naturalist . . . . _____
10. Outdoorsman . . . . _____
11. Scholar . . . . _____
12. Scientist . . . . _____
13. Showman . . . . _____
14. Sportsman . . . . _____
15. Traveler . . . . _____

WEBELOS AWARD
1. 10 years 9 months old . . . . _____
2. Tenderfoot requirements . . . _____
3. Visit troop meeting . . . . _____
4. Boy Scout application . . . . . _____
BADGE AWARDED . . . . _____

GRADUATION
Ceremony held . . . . _____
Date became Boy Scout . . . . _____

LEADERSHIP

	FROM	TO
Denner	_____	_____
Assistant denner	_____	_____

	FROM	TO
Webelos denner	_____	_____
Webelos asst. denner	_____	_____

MEMBERSHIP

Became Cub Scout (registered) . . . . _____
Joined Webelos den . . . . _____
Became Boy Scout (registered) . . . . _____

Transferred into pack . . . . _____
Transferred out of pack . . . . _____
Dropped from pack . . . . _____

17. UNIFORMS AND INSIGNIA

The moment a boy joins Cub Scouting—even before he becomes a member of your den—he's going to want the Cub Scout uniform. It gives him an immediate sense of belonging to an organized group.

The uniform is an obvious incentive to join Cub Scouting and, thus, is an aid in recruiting new boys. But its importance in Cub Scouting goes far beyond that, for it will help make the boy a better Cub Scout. It does this by:

♦ Reminding the boy to live up to the Cub Scout ideals.
♦ Drawing the attention of others and encouraging neat appearance and good behavior.
♦ Giving the boy the only proper place for display of his badges and other insignia.
♦ Encouraging the boy to stay on the Cub Scouting trail and graduate into Webelos Scouting and then Boy Scouting.

The Cub Scout uniform—and the Den Mother's, too—are in blue and gold. These colors have meaning in Cub Scouting, and the boys, their parents, and all Cub Scout leaders should know the meaning because it is a constant reminder of Cub Scouting's aims and ideals.

The **blue** stands for truth and spirituality, steadfast loyalty, and the sky above.

The **gold** stands for warm sunlight, good cheer, and happiness.

You and the other pack and den leaders should be properly uniformed at all Cub Scout events. Your good example of neat, correct uniforming will help inspire your Cub Scouts to proper dress at all pack and den meetings.

The Cub Scout uniform is made of sturdy, durable material designed to take the rough use it is likely to get in Cub Scouting activities. It may be worn almost anywhere—to church, school, or at play.

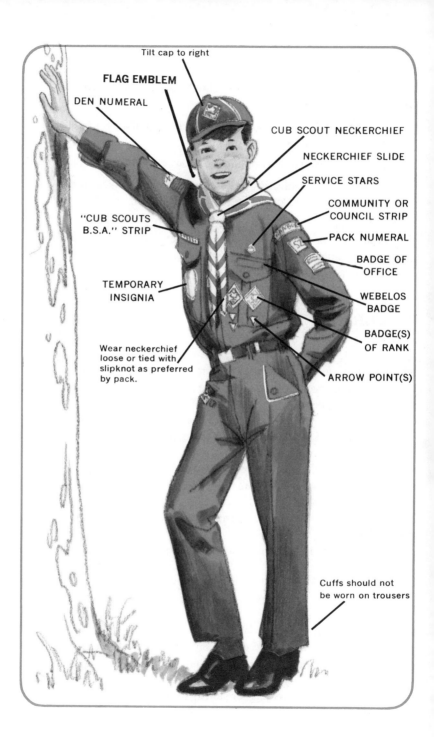

Tilt cap to right

FLAG EMBLEM

DEN NUMERAL

CUB SCOUT NECKERCHIEF

NECKERCHIEF SLIDE

SERVICE STARS

COMMUNITY OR COUNCIL STRIP

PACK NUMERAL

"CUB SCOUTS B.S.A." STRIP

BADGE OF OFFICE

TEMPORARY INSIGNIA

WEBELOS BADGE

BADGE(S) OF RANK

Wear neckerchief loose or tied with slipknot as preferred by pack.

ARROW POINT(S)

Cuffs should not be worn on trousers

WHEN THE UNIFORM
SHOULD NOT BE WORN

Neither Cub Scouts nor leaders should wear their uniforms when:

◆ Soliciting funds or engaging in any sales campaign to sell commercial products.

◆ Engaging in any distinctly political endeavor.

◆ Appearing on the stage professionally without special authority of the Executive Board of the National Council, Boy Scouts of America.

◆ Taking part in parades, except to render service as a Cub Scout or leader or when officially representing the Boy Scouts of America.

UNIFORMING YOUR DEN

While the Cub Scout uniform is not required of all boys, parents should be helped to see the great value in it. Boys naturally want to wear the uniform, and, when they do, their parents will find them more interested in the program. The uniform democratically dresses everyone on an equal basis. It gives boys a strong sense of belonging to a group and increases their feeling of security. It is a fundamental tool for building the interest of boys in the whole of Cub Scouting.

Suggest to parents that their son earns at least part of the cost of his uniform. Even an 8-year-old can do work around home to earn money toward a prized possession such as the uniform. This opportunity to teach habits of industry and thrift should not be missed.

If there is a boy in your den whose family simply cannot afford a uniform, tell your Cubmaster or pack committee. Probably they will be able to arrange for him to earn one.

Uniforms can be bought from stores that are official distributors for the Boy Scouts of America. Your Cubmaster will know where the nearest one is.

Now, let's look at both the Cub Scout and Den Mother's uniforms with the insignia each wears. Some of the same insignia are worn by both Cub Scouts and Den Mothers. Mothers of your Cub Scouts can find directions for sewing insignia on the uniform in the Wolf and Bear books.

THE NECKERCHIEF

Roll long edge tightly in several neat folds to about 6 inches from rear tip of the neckerchief. Place around neck of V-necked shirt or over collar of official long-sleeved shirt. (The collar of a long-sleeved shirt may be turned under when wearing the neckerchief.) Wear ends loose or in a slipknot as preferred by the pack.

BADGES OF IDENTIFICATION AND TENURE

Community and State Strips. The name of the community in which the chartered institution is located is embroidered with white lettering and border on a red background. The size is limited to 17 letters and spaces. Worn on the left sleeve of the uniform, centered below and touching the shoulder seam. The state strip is of the same embroidered pattern and is worn centered below and touching the community strip. Worn by all Cub Scouts and leaders.

"Cub Scouts B.S.A." Strip. Worn above the right shirt pocket seam. There is gold lettering on blue for Cub Scouts and Den Mothers and gold on khaki for Cub Scout leaders.

Pack Numeral. A white number, embroidered on a red background, worn centered on the left sleeve 2 inches below the shoulder seam. Worn by all Cub Scouts and leaders.

Flag Emblem. It may be worn by all Cub Scouts and leaders on the right sleeve, touching the shoulder seam. The Webelos Scout wears it over the right pocket.

Den Numeral. Gold letters and border, embroidered on a blue background, worn centered on the right sleeve 2 inches below the shoulder seam. Worn by Den Mothers and Cub Scouts.

Denner. Two gold stripes on a blue background worn centered on the left sleeve 4 inches below the shoulder seam. The denner stripes are worn only during term of office and then removed.

Assistant Denner. One gold stripe on a blue background is worn on the left sleeve and removed when term is completed.

Service Star. Cub Scouts may wear a plain star with gold background for each year of service or a single numbered star indicating total years of service. Worn centered over the left shirt pocket.

151

CUB SCOUT BADGES OF RANK

Bobcat. Badge of bronze-color metal. Worn centered on the left pocket of the Cub Scout uniform until the Wolf or a higher badge is worn. Then it must be removed.

Wolf. A cloth badge, black embroidered on a red background, worn on the left shirt pocket of the Cub Scout uniform. This design is the universal Cub Scout insignia appearing on buttons, caps, and belts.

Bear. A cloth badge, gold embroidered on a red background, worn on the left pocket of the Cub Scout uniform.

Arrow Points. Gold and silver embroidered cloth badges for the Wolf and Bear ranks elective program. Gold is for the first 10 credits earned; silver, for each additional 10 credits.

BADGES OF PARTICIPATION

Temporary Insignia. Temporary insignia may be authorized by local councils with the approval of the National Council to wear for a limited time or particular purpose in harmony with national policies. Not to exceed 3 inches in diameter. Cub Scouts wear it centered on the right shirt pocket. Den Mothers may wear it above the "CUB SCOUTS, B.S.A." strip.

Attendance Pin and Bar. Metal; gold color. Worn above left breast pocket of Cub Scout uniform. Bar is available for 2 to 10 years inclusive, to be added between 1-year bar and medal. Pack committee and leaders determine requirements. This insignia is not worn by adults.

DEN MOTHER'S UNIFORM

Your Den Mother's uniform is a trim, neat outfit appropriate for all den and pack activities. You will find that, when you participate in den activities in your uniform, the boys will accept you more readily as one of the group. It makes your relationship to the den more natural because all of you are in blue and gold.

Your wearing of the uniform also encourages the boys to wear theirs. It adds tremendously to the atmosphere and tone of the den and pack meeting. While it is true that the uniform requires an investment on your part, it is more suitable than other clothes for the type of activity that takes place in the dens.

Tilt cap to right

DEN MOTHER'S PIN

OFFICIAL TIE
(Gold with blue blouse
Blue with maize blouse)

SERVICE STARS

DEN MOTHER'S AWARD

TEMPORARY INSIGNIA

FLAG EMBLEM

"CUB SCOUTS
B.S.A." STRIP
(Worn with bottom even
with top of left pocket)

COMMUNITY OR
COUNCIL STRIP

PACK NUMERAL

DEN MOTHER'S BADGE

DEN NUMERAL

TRAINED STRIP

DEN MOTHER'S BLOUSE
(Navy blue or maize
as chosen by pack)

Do not wear
jewelry on uniform

**DEN MOTHER'S
UNIFORM**

Inspection Report

OF UNIFORM AND APPEARANCE
OF DEN MOTHERS

Den Mother:

Address:

District: _____ Pack No. ____ Den No. ____

PUT YOUR BEST FOOT FORWARD

Set a good example and encourage your boys to wear their uniforms correctly. Make sure your insignia are in the right places.

Encourage parents to check uniforms and insignia frequently, using charts on the inside front and back covers of the two Cub Scout handbooks.

Cap
Hostess style, navy blue with yellow piping. The Den Mother's pin is attached at the front on the left side. Cap is worn tilted to the right.

Blouse
1. Navy blue with short sleeves and roll collar, Dacron and cotton or twill—or
2. Maize with short sleeves and roll collar, Dacron and cotton or twill—or
3. Navy blue with long sleeves and roll collar.

Tie
1. A gold tie with a snap fastener. It is worn completely under the collar of the navy blue blouse with only the ends of the tie showing.
2. Navy blue tie, same style as above, worn in the same manner with the maize blouse.

Skirt
Navy blue with patch pockets, four-gored, flared.

Belt
Dark blue leather with a brass-tongue buckle.

Stockings and Shoes
Of personal choice.

Insignia
Den Mothers wear the blue "CUB SCOUTS B.S.A." strip with gold lettering, the den numeral, community strip, pack numeral, badge of office, and service stars on the Den Mother's blouse.

Assistant Den Mother wears an "Assistant" strip under the Den Mother badge.

BADGES OF IDENTIFICATION AND TENURE

Den Mother Pin and Badge. Metal badge is worn on the uniform cap or may be worn as a pin on civilian dress. The embroidered badge, gold on a dark blue background, is worn centered on the left sleeve of the blouse 4 inches below the shoulder seam.

Assistant Stripe. Worn directly under Den Mother badge by assistant Den Mothers. Blue letters on a gold background with blue border.

Service Star. Up to 10 years—A Den Mother may wear a single numbered star with light-blue background, indicating total years of service up to and including 10 years.

Over 10 years—For more than 10 years of service she may wear one star with a light-blue background with the numeral 10 or its multiples (20, 30, etc.) and a second star (1, 2, 3, etc.) indicating additional years up to the next multiple of 10. Worn centered over the left shirt pocket.

BADGES OF PARTICIPATION

Den Leader Badge. The Den Leader wears an embroidered badge, gold on khaki.

Den Leader's Training Award. A recognition for completing special training. It has the universal Boy Scout badge superimposed on the symbolic Cub Scout square suspended by a white ribbon with a narrow green stripe. Worn over the left shirt pocket.

Training Award Charm. The pendant of the Den Mother's Training Award is available to be worn at any time by a trained Den Mother on a bracelet or a necklace.

Training Award Pin. The pendant of the Den Leader's Training Award is available as a pin for civilian wear.

Square Knot. An embroidered badge of green and white on a khaki background may be worn in place of Den Mother's Training Award. Worn above left pocket of the blouse touching flap seam or just above blouse pocket, with service stars three-eighths of an inch above insignia.

Universal Scout Badge. Miniature, gold-color pin for civilian wear. May be worn by all registered personnel except Cub Scouts.

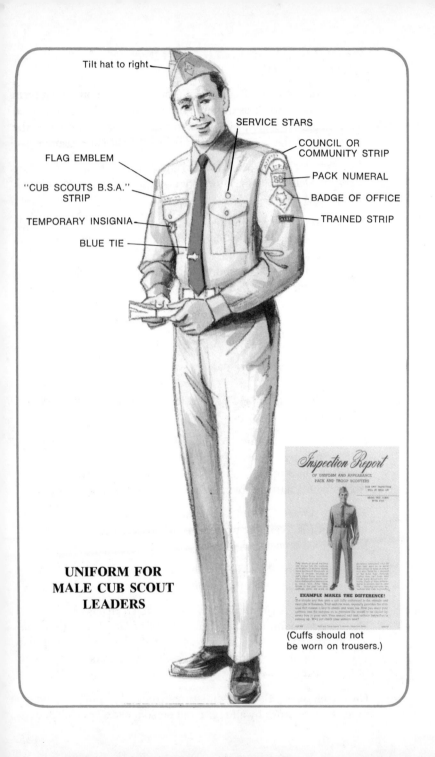

Tilt hat to right

SERVICE STARS

COUNCIL OR COMMUNITY STRIP

FLAG EMBLEM

PACK NUMERAL

"CUB SCOUTS B.S.A." STRIP

BADGE OF OFFICE

TEMPORARY INSIGNIA

TRAINED STRIP

BLUE TIE

UNIFORM FOR MALE CUB SCOUT LEADERS

Inspection Report

OF UNIFORM AND APPEARANCE, PACK AND TROOP SCOUTERS

EXAMPLE MAKES THE DIFFERENCE!

(Cuffs should not be worn on trousers.)

1. SERVICE STARS
2. COMMUNITY OR COUNCIL STRIP
3. PACK NUMERAL
4. ASSISTANT DENNER'S BADGE
5. BOBCAT BADGE
6. GOLD ARROW
   SILVER ARROW
7. WEBELOS BADGE
8. DENNER'S BADGE
9. DEN NUMERAL
10. FLAG EMBLEM

YOUR DEN CHIEF'S UNIFORM

Your den chief will wear his Boy Scout uniform to all den and pack activities. His leadership in Cub Scouting is indicated by the den chief's cord.

Two strands of blue cord interwoven with one of gold worn suspended from a blue, gold-bordered shoulder tab. Worn on the right shoulder of the Boy Scout uniform with the cord passing under the armpit. The den chief may wear Cub Scout service stars to indicate his years of service as a den chief. The shoulder tab without the cord may be worn with service stars to indicate past den chief service.

PART IV
WORKING WITH OTHERS

18. YOU AND YOUR DEN CHIEF

Y ou will get along better in your den if you understand from the very beginning that your den chief could be one of your problems. That's a perfectly natural situation. He is a key leader of the den and how he acts is bound to affect your den's performance. You will be off to a headstart on your job as Den Mother if you accept that as a fact.

There are important reasons for having a den chief in your den. Perhaps these reasons will help you to see this young den chief in a new light.

WHY HE IS IMPORTANT

First of all, the den chief can do things you cannot. He can participate actively in every type of game that a Cub Scout might play. He can teach the boys of your den to do many things that you would find difficult to do yourself. For instance, you might be hurt if you attempted to teach your boys to do the falling roll. It is not likely that you will find it fun to teach them to climb a rope either. Those things come naturally to a Boy Scout.

As you know, boys of Cub Scout age have heroes and secret ambitions. However, there is hardly a Cub Scout alive whose secret ambition it is to be a Den Mother! On the other hand, almost every 8- or 9-year-old boy would like to be 11 or 12. They would like to be Boy Scouts if they could. This means that the den chief already is what the Cub Scouts themselves would like to be. That puts him in an ideal position to give leadership. So that's another good reason why you will find him helpful.

A third reason why your den should have a den chief is that he serves as an ambassador from the Boy Scout troop. The den chief is an ever-present reminder to the boys that after their Webelos Scout year, the next step in Scouting is the troop.

HOW MUCH CAN YOU EXPECT
OF YOUR DEN CHIEF?

It will help you always to remember that your den chief is himself a boy. In many cases he is not much older than the members of your den. You won't be nearly so disturbed by some of the things he does if you expect him to act like a boy. If you expect his reactions and his leadership to be more adultlike than boyish, then you will be constantly dissatisfied.

Another thing to keep in mind is that your den chief considers himself to be a very busy young fellow. Even though he may be only a little older than the Cub Scouts, he'll have more homework to do, troop and patrol meetings to attend, sports to participate in and watch. One den chief, 14 years old, told his Den Mother that den activities were interfering with his social obligations. All of these things are important to boys of Boy Scout age. So don't be too disturbed if sometime he doesn't arrive on time at a den meeting. There will be times when he will even miss den meetings. If this happens too often, have a talk with him and suggest that prompt, regular attendance on his part is an example the Cub Scouts will emulate.

Your den chief's mind is filled with many important things. It might be unwise to expect him to remember from one week to the next to bring certain needed equipment to the den meeting. True, his intentions are excellent, but so is his ability to forget. Like Cub Scouts, themselves, he forgets better than he does many other things.

It was never intended that your den chief would plan your den meetings. You and the other adult pack leaders will do most of the den meeting planning. This is done at a regular pack leaders' meeting, which is explained in chapter 13. The Cubmaster or his assistant meets with the den chiefs regularly to pass along plans developed in the monthly pack leaders' meeting.

THE RIGHT WORKING RELATIONSHIP

More than any other thing, the success of your den chief will depend upon your working relationship with him. If you work together in a pleasant and friendly way, he will serve more effectively. He will also stay on the job for a longer time. He needs a satisfactory experience with you and the Cub Scouts if he is to continue.

While it is true that he is just a boy, he is beginning to feel a certain self-importance. Indeed, you must treat your den chief as a young man, even though inwardly you expect him to act like a boy. Make it clear to your den chief that you depend on him. He must feel that when you give him a job to do, you know it will be done. At the same time, when you give him an assignment, you must keep your weather eye on him to make certain that he does not get into difficulty. When he does, give him a helping hand. Do it in a way that makes it clear to him that you are only trying to be helpful.

Above all else, never humiliate your den chief by reprimanding or finding fault with him in front of the Cub Scouts. You see, they have put him on a pedestal. You will decrease the value of his leadership to the same degree that you lower him in the eyes of the Cub Scouts. The strength of his leadership will depend largely upon the extent to which you make him seem important and necessary to the den.

RECOGNITION IS IMPORTANT

There are many simple ways of recognizing your den chief. Even though you may be able to get along without his advice, there are occasions when you can ask it. This dignifies your relationship together. It helps him to feel that you need him and that you are working together as adults.

Of course, you will work with your Cubmaster to make sure that your den chief receives his den chief's shoulder cord and Den Chief's Warrant. These insignia of office are awarded by his Scoutmaster at an important troop occasion. There is a special way you can recognize your den chief with the Den Chief Appreciation Certificate, awarded at a pack meeting after he has served satisfactorily for a while. This is a colorful certificate that can be signed by the Cubmaster and leaders of the den. Your local council can help you to get copies of this award.

WHO IS THE BOSS?

Naturally no one would expect a boy of 12 or 13 to have final responsibility in the leadership of five or six active young boys. Such a responsibility requires mature judgment. In the final analysis you are responsible for your den and everything that goes on in it. Parents would not have confidence in Cub Scouting if this were not so.

This does not mean that you should do so much that the den chief is left with little to do. If this happens, he will not last long. You are responsible for leading and guiding the den chief and getting him to work with you as much as possible. On the other hand, the Den Mother who is content to sit back and let the den chief do all of the planning and leading is not likely to have a very satisfactory den.

You are the boss, but you will not be bossy. You will work in such a manner that the den chief feels it is a partnership. You will be as active as you find it necessary to be. But you will seize every opportunity to give the den chief a chance to lead, too!

DIVIDING THE DUTIES

How the den leadership duties are actually divided is a matter to be settled by you and the den chief. In general, the den chief leads the activities portion of your den meetings, especially the active games, tricks, puzzles, and stunts. He may also lead songs and have a hand in ceremonies.

If your den chief is an especially good leader, he might well take over the activities period entirely and leave you on the sidelines. This is particularly true if you can depend on your denner to give real help to the den chief.

What it boils down to is this: You're the captain of the ship; the den chief is your executive officer. The more responsibility you feel able to give him, the more likely he is to develop into a good leader. The more he is able to do, the less you'll have to do.

HOW IS THE DEN CHIEF RECRUITED?

The Scoutmaster is the leader who knows the most about the Scouts in his troop. Therefore, the Scoutmaster should share in the selection of den chiefs. It may be a great temptation for you to recruit your own den chief. Perhaps you have a fine Scout living near you, and you know that he would like to serve. Even so, it would not be wise for you to invite him to do so. His Scoutmaster may have other plans for him as a troop leader.

It is the responsibility of the Cubmaster and the Scoutmaster to work together in recruiting den chiefs. This brings about better cooperation between the pack and the troop and helps the Scoutmaster to understand that the den chief is really a troop leader representing the troop in the pack. So, if you need a den chief, get in touch with your Cubmaster; he will work out a solution with the Scoutmaster. He will confer with you before a definite assignment is made. The Application To Become a Den Chief will help in making the best choice.

HOW LONG SHOULD A DEN CHIEF SERVE?

There is no definite length of time that we can expect a den chief to serve. It will depend upon the individual boy. If he is busy with many other things, his term will be shorter. On the other hand, if he has an especially pleasant relationship, this will help offset the pull of other interests.

Urge your den chief to serve as long as possible. It will make your job easier, and the den will run more smoothly.

TO GET A DEN CHIEF

1. Tell your Cubmaster you need one.
2. Cubmaster discusses your need with Scoutmaster.
3. Scoutmaster selects right boy trained in leadership skills.
4. Cubmaster trains him in Cub Scouting skills.

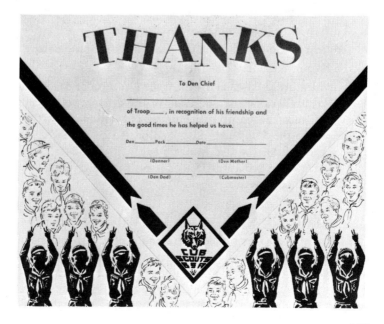

19. YOU AND THE DEN LEADER COACH

There's no doubt at all that you will find in your job as Den Mother that the Den Leader coach is your best friend.

Why? Simply because the Den Leader coach has only one reason for existence in a Cub Scout pack: to help you.

In most packs, the Den Leader coach will be a woman, probably an experienced former Den Mother, but men also may serve as Den Leader coaches. If your pack is new and has no former Den Mothers to call upon, a man or woman might be selected from among the pack's organizers and given special training to serve as Den Leader coach.

THE DEN LEADER COACH'S DUTIES

The Den Leader coach has three prime duties:

1. To give immediate training to new Den Mothers.
2. To help all Den Mothers in the pack with their problems.
3. To help in recruiting Den Mothers.

It's evident from this summary that the Den Leader coach can have a great effect on the operation of the dens in your pack. The Den Leader coach also tries to aid in recruiting new Cub Scouts, keeps the Cubmaster informed on the condition of the dens, suggests ideas for Den Mothers to try in their dens, helps with den records, encourages Den Mothers to take training, and promotes den parents' meetings.

HOW THE DEN LEADER COACH WORKS

If you are a new Den Mother, the Den Leader coach will make an appointment to visit you in your home and explain how Cub Scouting works and what the Den Mother's role is.

This visit will be an informal, friendly coaching affair before your first den meeting. This will give you an idea of what to ex-

pect. The coach can help you decide on a den meeting place in your home, and she may have some suggestions on how to set it up and what you'll need.

The coach will explain the seven parts of the den meeting and why each is important, and will also help you plan the details of your first meeting. The Den Leader coach will be delighted to answer any questions you might have before your first meeting concerning where you can get ideas, how to use such literature as the *Cub Scout Program Helps, Scouting Magazine,* and *Boys' Life* magazine, and how the advancement plan works.

As a result of this visit, you ought to absorb a great deal of basic Cub Scout methods and practices. Undoubtedly, the Den Leader coach will offer to come to your first den meeting and help with it if necessary. The coach might even attend the second if you feel you need help.

The sole aim of the coach in all this is to get you started with confidence and some knowledge of Cub Scouting.

HELPING ALL THE DEN MOTHERS

Whether you are facing your first den meeting or are a veteran of 6 months or even a year or two as Den Mother, the Den Leader coach may be helpful to you. Especially, if she has had long-and-successful experience as a Den Mother, she will be able to offer ideas and suggestions on your den problems.

The Den Leader coach helps all Den Mothers in your pack in two ways:

◆ By regular monthly meetings, usually after the pack leaders' meeting.

◆ By conferring with individual Den Mothers at any time.

During the regular monthly pack leaders' meetings, the Den Leader coach and the Cubmaster work on detailed plans for each of your den meetings for the next month.

After that meeting, most Den Leader coaches hold a meeting of all Den Mothers in the pack, primarily to work out the specific details for each Den Mother's four den meetings. This is also the time when she may suggest new ideas for den activities, how to handle the problem boy, discipline in general, recordkeeping, using the pack library, the need for den parents' meetings. In fact, anything that might be helpful to the pack's Den Mothers.

This is also the time for you to bring up den problems, except such things as handling a particular problem boy. That type of personal problem might best be left for a conference of the Den Leader coach and you alone.

If the Den Leader coach is an old hand at Cub Scouting, her practical suggestions on all of these den problems can be invaluable to you. The coach will know the type of activities that work and which ones don't, will have experience with discipline problems, and will know how to plan activities that combine the fun of Cub Scouting and its serious purposes.

THE DEN LEADER COACH AND THE PACK

The Den Leader coach serves as the Cubmaster's "right-hand man" in dealing with the dens. She (or he) is appointed by the Cubmaster and approved for the job by the pack committee.

In most packs the coach will be the recruiter of Den Mothers, although this job remains the responsibility of the Cubmaster. The coach may have recruited you and then met with you, the Cubmaster, and the other parents in your den when the former Den Mother left the den.

The coach has no direct responsibilities at pack meetings, but will be there to offer help to any Den Mother who needs it then or at any other time.

20. YOU AND THE PARENTS

Cub Scouting is a family program. If you have read through the book to this point, it is clear to you that most of a boy's experience in Cub Scouting is in the den and in his own home.

It is obvious, then, that the parents play a big part in their son's activities as a Cub Scout. It's safe to say that if his parents ignore his Cub Scout activities, then he won't enjoy real Cub Scouting at all.

Parents who go all out to help their sons will be involved in many phases of Cub Scouting, both in the den and the pack. But there are two basic things they *must* do if their son is to get the best of his Cub Scout experience:
1. Help him with his achievements and electives.
2. Attend the monthly pack meetings, especially when their son is to receive a badge or an award.

Without at least this much help and encouragement, almost certainly a boy will be cheated out of a great deal that Cub Scouting can offer him simply because so much of the program concerns his home and the help of his family.

Aside from the fact that probably you are a Cub Scout's parent yourself, just what does this mean to you? What can you do as a Den Mother to help make Cub Scouting the home-centered program it is meant to be?

THE RIGHT START

The first rule of parent participation is to make sure that no boy joins your pack and den until you have made clear to his parents their responsibility toward Cub Scouting. It won't be easy to say "no" to an enthusiastic 8-year-old who rings your doorbell. However, you will do him a real service if you tell him you must discuss the matter with his parents before you consider his membership as a Cub Scout.

Very often boys become Cub Scouts before their parents fully understand the program. We have no basis for complaining about lack of parent interest if we do not make clear to parents just what we expect of them.

When a new boy wants to join your den, invite him and his parents to a pack meeting. Give them a copy of *Cub Scouting and a Boy*. Arrange for the Cubmaster, your den dad, or another pack committeeman to call upon his parents and explain how the program works. (You might go along if you can.)

They will make certain that the parents know they are expected to attend monthly pack meetings. They will explain the advancement program and make it clear that parents are expected to work with their son on his achievements.

The best time to get a pledge of parent cooperation is when they want their sons to join.

One of the best and easiest ways to do all this is for the Cubmaster or other leader to use the *Cub Scout Parent Orientation Flip Chart* and the parent supplements in the front of Wolf and Bear books and also explain the Application To Join a Pack.

HOW TO GET PARENTS TO HELP

You need not be apologetic when you ask parents to cooperate with you. After all, you're asking them to do things for their own boys. You gain nothing personally from their cooperation. Their boys gain everything. Parents understand this, and that places you in an excellent position for requesting their help.

Some Den Mothers are disturbed because parents do not ask if they can help in some way. Really, it just isn't natural for parents to do that. They simply take it for granted that if their help is needed you will ask for it.

One of the things you must keep in mind then is that the best way to get help is to look as if you can't get along without it. There is no point in becoming disturbed over this. It's just natural for folks to sit back and let you do the job alone if it looks as if you're able to do it.

In Cub Scouting we call this "leaning." We have found out that if you lean hard enough in the direction of other folks, they will help to hold you up. It's a matter of balance. The object is to lean just enough so that you have other folks supporting you all along the line. And remember, make absolutely clear the kind of help you need. Parents will respond if you make your requests definite.

WOLF PARENTS' SUPPLEM

BEAR PARENTS' SUPPLEME

WEBELOS PARENTS' SUPPLEMENT

BOY SCOUTS

BOY SCOU

1

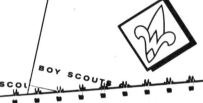

PURPOSE

ACHIEVEMENT

FAMILY FUN

Copyright 1963
BOY SCOUTS OF A
New Brunswick   N
No. 4343

Cub Scouting
and a
Boy

WHEN YOUR BOY IS 8 OR 9

WHEN YOUR BOY IS 10

CUB SCOUT PARENT ORIENTATION FLIP CHART

FOR USE BY
- Pack Committeemen
- Cubmasters
- Assistant Cubmasters

WITH
New Cub Scout Parents

WAYS PARENTS CAN HELP

Since your success in working with parents will depend upon whether you give them definite things to do, here are a few of the ways in which they can help you.

HELPING WITH DEN MEETINGS.—While you and the den chief are able to run the den meetings, nevertheless it's a good idea to get other parents to help. It keeps them interested and makes your job easier.

You might develop a schedule so that each mother knows she has a specific meeting to attend. If you and the parents believe that your boys should have refreshments, then it should be the assisting mother's responsibility to bring and serve them. She should also help you in every way possible with the actual den meeting. Perhaps if you have younger children, she can manage them for you.

Mothers are usually very willing to cooperate in such a plan. If there are seven boys in the den, for example, each mother must come to a den meeting only once every 6 or 7 weeks. That isn't much for you to ask.

There are many advantages to this plan, but the most important is that it gets all mothers interested in the den. It's excellent training. When it becomes necessary for you to discontinue your service as a Den Mother, all of the other mothers of the den will have had some valuable experience and it will be easier to recruit your successor. Of course, if you have a regular assistant Den Mother, she would be the logical candidate.

WITH THE ADVANCEMENT PROGRAM.—You need the help of all parents in working with their boys on the advancement program. Most difficulties that arise in the passing of achievements in the home are due to lack of understanding by the parents.

See chapter 15 for details on how parents help in advancement.

WITH DEN PROJECTS.—In almost every month of the year you need the help of parents in connection with the projects on which your den is working. You generally find that parents are happy to have a part in these projects if they understand them clearly and realize how they can help. If the project is of a type that requires cooperation from the dads, call upon the den dad to work with the men. If it is the cooperation of mothers that you need, then you or the assistant Den Mother can ask them to help. Perhaps in the fall you want to fix up a better indoor meeting place

for your den. The den dad can help by getting other dads to assist. It would be grand to get each dad and boy to make a bench or chair. Dads enjoy this sort of activity, provided they understand what is wanted.

Perhaps the theme for the month requires simple costumes for the den stunt. Mothers and dads will help with props and costumes if you ask them. Naturally, you must keep your demands within reason. If it is simple and doesn't involve great expense, you will have no difficulty.

WITH PACK MEETINGS.—The first obligation of every parent is to attend the monthly pack meeting.

In addition to attending the pack meeting, parents may be asked occasionally to make some contribution to it. Sometimes your den exhibits or stunts will require the help of a number of the dads in the den.

WITH SUMMER ACTIVITIES.—Parents can help keep your den active in the summertime by assisting with den and pack activities. They can help your pack earn the National Summertime Pack Award as well as help your den qualify for the den participating ribbon. See chapter 13 for details.

WITH PACK FINANCES.—The parents can help with pack finances by making sure their son pays his dues promptly each week. Suggest that parents provide ways for their sons to earn the small amount needed for their dues. This will help teach the boys the value of money and the importance of discharging financial obligations.

Make sure your den parents understand how the pack budget works, in general if not in detail.

DEN PARENTS' MEETINGS

One of the best ways to keep the parents of your den interested is to hold two den parents' meetings each year. Get several of the mothers to assist you with this meeting. They can help with refreshments and with getting attendance. Cub Scouts do not attend these meetings.

Give parents an opportunity to learn how the den is getting along. Share your problems with them. Give them a chance to make suggestions for den activities. When a parent suggests one, get that parent to run it.

Discuss the advancement program with the parents. Show them how to use it effectively in their own homes. Invite the Cubmaster to attend in order that he may present some phase of Cub Scouting to them.

You'll find that this sort of meeting develops den spirit in the parents. They'll pride themselves on the things your den is attempting to do.

A den parents' meeting ought to be very informal. The scene probably is your home some evening after dinner. It's a good idea to make a few notes of things you want to cover with the parents. Encourage discussion and exchange of ideas. This is a fine time to involve more parents in the work of your den.

It can be an especially important conference, if your pack does not hold separate meetings of parents at each pack meeting; because it gives you a chance to discuss with the parents, not only the pack and den's plans and problems, but also the basic aims of Cub Scouting. Make the most of it.

THE DEN DAD AND THE PARENTS

The den dad's duties have been explained elsewhere in the book; but it seems appropriate to mention him again here, because so much of his work is bound up with the other den parents.

So far as your den is concerned, perhaps his most important duty is to get the other fathers to attend pack meetings. He should keep in close touch with the other fathers, reminding them about pack meetings and urging them to take part in special den events for fathers and sons. He is your liaison with half your den parents —the fathers.

21. YOUR TRAINING OPPORTUNITY

There are two very good reasons why you are going to be interested in having some training experience. The first is that you can serve as Den Mother or Den Leader with less time and effort if you are trained to do your job. It is usually a great deal harder to do a thing the wrong way than the right way, and the results are far more satisfying when you do it the right way.

In addition to saving your time, training will give you greater confidence. It will show you how to work with your den in such a way that the experience will be as fine as possible for you and your boys. There are tricks in any trade, and the main purpose of Den Leader training is to give you the tricks you will need.

For information about training opportunities, ask your Den Leader coach, Cubmaster, or the local council office. The council office tries to make it as easy as possible for you to take training; the training plan is such that it can be adapted to almost any situation.

There are several ways that training can be provided:

1. Den Mothers or Den Leaders and prospective Den Mothers or Den Leaders of a single pack may get together.
2. Den Mothers or Den Leaders of neighboring packs may get together.
3. A Den Leaders' training course can be set up for all packs of a district.
4. Personal coaching may be provided by your Den Leader coach.

DEN LEADER TRAINING

There are four training sessions the Den Mothers or Den Leaders must take in order to complete their training. These, plus participation in a Cub Scout leaders' pow wow, will help you become an effective leader. The four training sessions and the pow wow are outlined below. Each subject is complete within itself and includes not only information about one phase of Cub Scouting but also practical program material for ceremonies,

songs, games, and crafts. These training sessions also provide an excellent opportunity for you to meet and exchange ideas with other Den Leaders. If you are new, it is especially important to know how other leaders began their training and are making use of it in their den programs.

THE CUB SCOUT PROGRAM—AN ORIENTATION SESSION.—This training session is designed to orient leaders and parents of prospective or new Cub Scouts. It will help you as a Den Mother or Den Leader to understand how the Cub Scout program works. You will gain needed information about the Cub Scout advancement plan and pick up valuable hints on how to help parents work it into the natural activities of their boys. You will see how to fit achievements into your den program.

By having mothers and fathers attend this orientation session with you, you can ensure better parent participation in your den. It will help them to understand better their Cub Scout-age boy and how Cub Scouting activities and the advancement plan can help him. As parents understand the purpose of the Cub Scout program, they will become more cooperative and enthusiastic.

During this orientation session, you will learn how the den and pack are organized and how leaders and parents work effectively togther to make the ideals important and meaningful.

PLANNING THE CUB SCOUT PROGRAM.—This training session covers program planning in the den and pack. It includes an explanation of how to accomplish the three steps in program planning: how to get program planning under way, the responsibility of all leaders involved in program planning, and what makes a good theme. You will have a chance to see how pack and den meetings are planned, using this book, the *Cub Scout Program Helps, Cub Scout Leader's Program Notebook, Boys' Life,* and other literature.

You will learn the Cubmaster's and the pack committee's relationship to den and pack meeting programs. You will learn how you are related to other leaders in the planning of these programs. Best of all, you will discover that under proper program planning methods you are not expected to plan all of your den meeting programs on your own.

THE DEN MEETING.—In this session you will be taken step by step through a typical den meeting program. You will learn about the seven parts of a den meeting and why each is important.

This is not a lecture experience, but one in which you will participate in some typical den meeting activities. By the time the session is completed, you will have participated in a model den meeting program and will have many ideas and activities for each of the seven parts of a den meeting to use with your den.

OPERATING A DEN.—When Den Mothers or Den Leaders understand fully how to work with and use their den chiefs, they will find that they will make a great contribution to the smooth operation of the dens. This training session will give you an idea of what you can expect of your den chief. It will also suggest some things that you should not expect him to do. Most important, it will show you how to work with him most effectively in dealing with the boys of your den.

It will also cover securing and using a den chief, how to involve parents, using the den dad, meeting the needs of boys, handling discipline problems, as well as the right approach to financial matters.

CUB SCOUT LEADERS' POW WOW

The pow wow is an annual fun-filled training experience for all pack leaders and prospective leaders—the Cubmaster, Den Mothers, Den Leaders, and pack committeemen.

When they attend a pow wow, Den Mothers and Den Leaders participate in the Games, Crafts, or Skits and Puppets sections. After completing one of these sections, they receive credit for the training requirements toward the Den Leader's Training Award.

DEN LEADER'S TRAINING AWARD

The Den Leader's Training Award is a means of recognizing a Den Mother or Den Leader or assistants who are trained and give consistent service to the Cub Scout program. It stands for a high standard of performance. The award is available to all registered Den Mothers or Den Leaders and assistants.

The requirements include: (1) completion of the four Den Leader training sessions outlined on pages 178-81 and participation in a pow wow; (2) tenure—2 consecutive years as a registered Den Mother or Den Leader or assistant, or 1 year as assistant Den Mother or Den Leader and 1 year as Den Mother or Den Leader; (3) performance—this means that you will have to demonstrate leadership responsibility by doing the following:

(a) accept and perform leadership responsibility in Cub Scouting for at least three den meetings a month, (b) earn the National Summertime Pack Award; (c) show that you have a den chief who meets regularly with your den; (d) plan and conduct, at least once a year, a successful meeting for parents of boys in your den; and do two additional projects of those listed:

♦ Serve on a project committee for four outdoor pack activities.

♦ Build or assemble a den game chest—submit list of equipment.

♦ Supervise or counsel a den in furnishing and equipping a den meeting place.

♦ Participate with other adult pack leaders in at least 16 monthly pack leaders' meetings.

PART V
DEN LEADER'S LORE

22. HISTORY OF CUB SCOUTING

A s a Den Mother or Den Leader, you stand in the ranks of more than 350,000 men and women across all America who lead Cub Scout dens. They have in their charge more than 2 million Cub Scouts.

That's a lot of men and women and a lot of boys, and the great size of this Cub Scout family attests to the vitality and universal appeal of the Cub Scout program.

When and where did it all begin? Well, Cub Scouting was launched experimentally in the United States in 1929, but its roots go back even further. Its beginnings can be traced to 1908 when a book called *Scouting for Boys* was published in England.

To start our story, we'll go back to the turn of the century when an English Army officer who was stationed in India felt the need for a method of teaching his men resourcefulness, adaptability, and the qualities of leadership demanded by frontier conditions. This officer was Col. Robert S. S. Baden-Powell. He wrote a handbook called *Aids to Scouting*—scouting with a small "s" in the sense of reconnaissance.

Serving in South Africa in 1899, Baden-Powell achieved world fame during the Boer War by holding the small town of Mafeking for 217 days against an enemy force 10 times as great as his own.

When he returned to England as a military hero, promoted to major general, he was amazed to find that his little handbook had caught the imagination of English boys. The game of "scouting" was being played by the youth of England.

Baden-Powell had the vision and the social sense to see the possibilities of his idea for youth. Drawing heavily upon memories of his own experiences, and upon youth programs of ancient and modern countries, he developed a program and wrote a handbook for it. This appeared in 1908 as the now world-famous book *Scouting for Boys*. It revealed a warm understanding of boys and what they like to do. Instead of curbing their gang spirit, Scouting encouraged them to play under leaders of their own choosing.

BOY SCOUTS
OF
AMERICA

BY
ERNEST
THOMPSON
SETON
AND
LIEUT·GEN·
ERAL SIR
ROBERT S.S.
BADEN·
POWELL
K.C.B.

OFFICIAL HANDBOOK

PRICE 25 CENTS NET

EARLY AMERICAN ORIGINS

About this same time, the seeds of Scouting were germinating in the rich pioneering tradition of America. Indians and heroes of the frontier were a part of every boy's life, whether he lived in the country or in the city. In this hero worship, thoughtful leaders saw an opportunity for developing qualities of independence and resourcefulness, as well as skills in nature lore and outdoor activities.

Two youth organizations that were developing at this time in the United States were Ernest Thompson Seton's Woodcraft Indians, based on Indian lore; and Daniel Carter Beard's Sons of Daniel Boone, featuring the pioneers. Both organizations required an intimate knowledge and love of the outdoors.

Thus by 1910 there were somewhat similar youth movements both in England and in the United States, although at this time Baden-Powell's Boy Scout movement was better organized, and its program was richer in spiritual values.

UNKNOWN SCOUT'S GOOD TURN

On a foggy night in London, an American businessman was seeking a certain address. A boy approached and asked if he might help. Having escorted the American personally to the address, the boy courteously refused a tip, saying he was a Scout and could not receive payment for a Good Turn.

The man was William D. Boyce, a Chicago publisher, and the story of his interest in Scouting growing out of this incident is now a highlight of Scouting history.

After further investigation, Mr. Boyce brought back to America an enthusiasm for Scouting and a trunkful of pamphlets. He incorporated the Boy Scouts of America on February 8, 1910. Shortly, thereafter, a group of public-spirited citizens set up an organization. They appointed James E. West as executive officer of the movement.

The Boy Scouts of America grew by leaps and bounds. A Federal Charter was granted to it by Congress in 1916—an honor extended to few organizations.

But whether in the United States or abroad, Scouting is rooted in the history of mankind. Today it is a world brotherhood bound together by a common Oath or Promise and ideals. Scouting has a language understandable by all—a love for nature, a fellowship for man, and a respect for God who created both.

The first official Cub Scout uniform consisted of knickers, long socks, cap, and the option of shirt or sweater.

CUB SCOUTING BACKGROUND

The Cub Scout program of the Boy Scouts of America was carefully built as a direct answer to the demands of millions of boys of Cub Scout age and their parents, who, as early as 1911, were calling for their own program.

Wolf Cubbing started in England in 1914 when Baden-Powell started to experiment with a program for younger boys based on Kipling's "The Jungle Book." In 1916 he made a public announcement of this program, and since that time it has spread with very little change into the other European countries.

At the First National Training Conference of American Scout Executives in 1920, the needs of the young boys were emphasized, but the National Council felt it wise to defer action until they had more objective evidence. In 1925 a research psychologist was authorized to study what was already being done in the way of a suitable program for younger boys and to explore general interest at various age levels. His recommendation indicated that younger boys responded even better to leadership and program efforts than boys of Boy Scout age.

SCIENTIFIC BASIS

In 1926 the Executive Board of the National Council authorized the Chief Scout Executive to proceed with a plan for raising $50,000 for a thorough scientific study of the whole younger-boy matter. In 1927 an advisory committee was appointed, composed of top specialists in the fields of child psychology, family life, etc., to cooperate with the Boy Scouts of America in developing this program. At this time the Laura Spelman Rockefeller Foundation made available the $50,000 necessary to carry on the basic study, to develop a plan, and to produce the necessary literature.

In addition to the committees already mentioned, advice was sought at various steps in the development of the program from more than 13,500 leading psychologists, sociologists, teachers, school superintendents, professors of education, college executives, and recreation and welfare directors.

The Executive Board approved a plan of experimenting in a limited number of communities, and on August 1, 1929, the first demonstration units were started. In 1930, the Cub Scout program was formally launched with 5,102 boys registered at the end of that year. During the next 3 years, a close study of these experimental groups was made so that definite experience might be used as a basis for the final development of a program. By 1933 it was felt the time had come to promote Cub Scouting as a part of the Boy Scout program throughout the country, and the experimental restrictions were removed. In 1935, William C. Wessel was appointed the first director of Cub Scouting.

For more than a decade the English Wolf Cub plan had been tried in America along with a score of other programs. Quite uniformly, there was difficulty in keeping activities different from those of the Boy Scout troop, thus taking the edge off the boy's later experience as a Boy Scout.

Our Cub Scout program corrected this. It is different from the younger-boy programs of any other country in the world because it is home- and neighborhood-centered and is built around between-meeting activities. The program suggests a wide range of attractive things for the Cub Scout and his play group to do with the encouragement of parents and neighbors. It suggests things that youngsters enjoy doing on their own when not under adult direction. These activities are particularly suited to the boy of Cub Scout age and must be kept quite different from those he will encounter at 11 years of age.

Cub Scouting in our country has drawn upon the dramatic lore and lure of the American Indian for program background. Its Promise and Law were drafted with the advice of educators who were specialists in dealing with boys of these ages. Many handicrafts were developed in recognition that this period is an opportune time to develop skills.

The system of electives was instituted to force practice in making decisions as well as to take into account individual differences among boys. Cub Scouting's objective is, through its advancement plan and program, to deliver a graduating Cub Scout, stimulated and prepared to participate in the Boy Scout program.

The Laura Spelman Rockefeller Foundation and the Boy Scouts of America were determined that this new Cub Scout program meet the needs of the American family. In this, as more than 35 years of experience have shown, they succeeded!

23. HELPS FOR YOU

The books, pamphlets, and other helps described here are only a few of the many that will help you plan exciting and interesting den and pack activities and orient parents.

They should be included in your Den Mother's kit and in your pack library. Ask your Cubmaster about obtaining them. The numbers with most of these publications are catalog numbers to help in ordering them.

FOR PROGRAM IDEAS

Cub Scout Program Helps is perhaps the most fertile source of ideas you will find. It is mailed in segments in *Scouting Magazine* to all Cubmasters, Den Mothers, Den Leaders, Webelos den leaders, and Den Leader coaches and assistants.

Cub Scout Program Helps is rich in den and pack program material based on a suggested theme for the month and the Webelos activity badge areas. You will find practical games, ceremonies, tricks and puzzles, craftwork, skits and stunts, and ideas for each den meeting. You can create a storehouse of ideas as a part of your den library kit by starting a three-ring binder of these to pass on to your successor.

The *Wolf Cub Scout Book,* No. 3207, and *Bear Cub Scout Book,* No. 3208, are designed for the 8- and 9-year-old boy, respectively. Each book includes projects, activities, crafts, and requirements Cub Scouts complete to earn the Wolf or Bear badge and the arrow points for each. They will give you ideas for program activity in your den and will help you with information on crafts, ceremonies, games, and skills.

The *Cub Scout Leader's Program Notebook* and Pack Program Planning Chart are published annually.

In addition, you will find helpful pages to be used in planning your den meeting programs. You will find it particularly helpful to have the notebook available at your monthly pack leaders' meetings and roundtables.

Boys' Life is the monthly magazine for all boys published by the Boy Scouts of America. Besides a host of good stories and articles, each issue includes special features and "how-to-do-its" based on the monthly Cub Scout theme.

Cub Scout Songbook, No. 3221, is packed with songs your Cub Scouts will enjoy singing. It includes greeting songs, fellowship songs, fun songs, lively songs, action songs, advancement and graduation songs, and farewell songs.

It would be helpful to have a supply of these books in your den meeting place. The books help the boys to learn the songs more quickly.

Cub Scout Activities, No. 4525, is filled with ideas for year-round den activities. It will guide you in a complete den program with the emphasis on outdoor den fun wherever you live.

Cub Scout Water Fun, No. 3220, is designed especially for dads of boys of Cub Scout age. This handy book will help you plan a program that will attract and use den dads in giving their boys training in swimming and water skills.

Staging Den and Pack Ceremonies, No. 3214, contains a collection of tried-and-tested den and pack ceremonies of all kinds. This book will be valuable to you in planning your own den ceremonies, making props, and participating in pack ceremonies. The ceremonies are grouped so that you can easily select the ones to fit your needs.

Cub Scout Magic, No. 3219, contains a variety of tricks, puzzles, and stunts for den and pack meetings. This book tells and shows boys how they can be real Cub Scout magicians. It is an excellent source of ideas for your den meeting gathering-time activities.

Group Meeting Sparklers, No. 3122, is loaded with icebreakers, mixers and group-participation, action, and applause stunts designed to pep up meetings. You will find this book an excellent source of ideas to add life and fun to your activities.

Games for Cub Scouts, No. 3844, is filled with den and pack games of all types. Your Cub Scouts will enjoy playing the traditional, circle, fitness, observation, relay, and other types of challenging indoor and outdoor games. This book will help you plan games and make equipment and props for your den games.

Crafts for Cub Scouts, No. 3843, is filled with simple how-to-do-it projects. It will help you use paper, wood, leather, plastic, metal, and other materials in your den crafts. It includes workable plans for gifts, household novelties, and practical items for boys and parents.

Skits and Puppets, No. 3842, offers a complete assortment of activities for den and pack meetings. It will show you how to make puppets; put on shows; write skits; and make stages, costumes, and props. It also includes scripts for shows and stunts relating to the theme of the month.

Webelos Den Activities, No. 3853, is packed with ideas for the Webelos den leader to use in conducting his weekly meetings based on Webelos activity badges. It will show him how to set up demonstrations and displays and how to use outside help.

Den Chief's Denbook, No. 3211, outlines the responsibilities of the den chief and explains his part in assisting you to hold better den meetings. It includes a variety of games, tricks, ceremonies, and crafts to help him to do his job.

FOR PARENT ORIENTATION

Guidebook to Cub Scouting, No. 3822, presents briefly the story of Cub Scouting—its purposes, organization, and how it works. It is especially helpful for use with parents who wish their boys to become members of your den.

The parent supplements in the Wolf and Bear books are excellent tools for informing parents *why* and *how* they should participate with their sons in Cub Scouting. The supplement in the Wolf book should be read by every Cub Scout family when the son starts working on his Wolf badge, and the supplement in the Bear book while he is 9. In fact, a condition of membership might be the reading of the pamphlet by both parents.

Cub Scout Parent Orientation Flip Chart, No. 4185, is designed to guide pack leaders in outlining to parents of new Cub Scouts what Cub Scouting means to their boy and how they can help. Ask your Cubmaster to use it with the parents of new boys coming into your den.

Here is a list of other publications and forms mentioned in this book, with their catalog numbers.

National Tour Permit Application, No. 4419

Local Tour Permit Application, No. 4426

Application To Become a Den Chief, No. 4211

Cub Scout Application, No. 28-109

Cub Scout Fun Book, No. 3215

Individual Cub Scout Record, No. 3827

Den Advancement Report, No. 3847

Cub Scout Advancement Chart, No. 4189

Replacement sheets for No. 4189, No. 4190

Den Mother Appreciation Certificate, No. 3754

Den Chief's Warrant, No. 3727

Cub Scout Den Record, No. 3828

Den Chief Appreciation Certificate, No. 4223

Monthly Den Dues Envelope, No. 4209

Unit Money-Earning Application, No. 4427

Weekly Den Dues Envelope, No. 4210

Weekly Den Meeting Program, No. 3826

Cub Scouting and a Boy, No. 3829

How To Be a Den Chief, No. 6453

INDEX